A Styal Of Its Own

(1894-1964)

by

James Stanhope-Brown

A STYAL OF ITS OWN

INTRODUCTION

This story was born from a natural desire to trace the roots of a childhood which was mysteriously entrenched behind the gates of Manchester's largest orphan colony at Styal. Like the many thousands who served out their childhood in an isolation away from civilisation, I was curious to learn the facts surrounding this unique experience.

As a result of my efforts which somehow evolved into a 'yesteryear type' heritage revelation, I was able to produce a story which not only answered the many questions based on childhood inquisitiveness, but also one which provided answers to years of doubt and uncertainty.

Since the village of Styal and the Greg's of Quarry Bank Mill were participants of this story, it was only natural that local historical detail in connection with 'A Styal of its Own' would be highlighted. Therefore, I would like to take this opportunity of offering my apologies to anyone who feels that my observations have been unfair. Any bias is completely unintentional. — Just the English Grammar is painful.

Finally, this book is dedicated to all those former children of circumstance who spent their childhood at the Styal Colony.

ACKNOWLEDGEMENTS

Wilmslow Public Library

Wilmslow Parish Church

Quarry Bank Mill, Styal

Manchester Public Library - Archives and Local History

Manchester Evening News

The Wilmslow Advertiser

Withington Hospital - Tony Thorlby, Keith Harrison

The Toronto Star Newspaper

Manchester Town Hall

The publication of this book has only been made possible due to the interest and kind generosity of Mrs Christine Pothecary, a descendent of the Mottershead family whose roots span two centuries of Styal's history.

Published by: Christine Pothecary

Typesetting by: Sarah Macdonald

Printed by MFP Design & Print 0161- 864 4540

ISBN No. 0/9515652/0/6

Chapter One

DESTINY

The village of Styal and its destiny was mapped out by two men, both of whom, choosing the locality for different purposes. With a professionalism each to his own trade, they came to Styal with one aim in mind. Each found what they were looking for and each left his mark on a Cheshire beauty spot which had lain undisturbed for hundreds of years. Yet, at the precise moment in time, the village awoke to its calling and adapted to its preordained destiny and it's new masters. The first and most enterprising of the two men of history was Samuel Greg, who started his first cotton spinning mill at Quarry Bank, during the year 1784. Doctor Rhodes, the lesser known and Salford born doctor of medicine, adopted Styal for his 'orphan colony', just one hundred and ten years later. In terms of size , Styal represents not much more than four square miles, yet within an era of 170 years, historical drama flowed in and out of the village like the old meandering River Bollin. Fate and destiny both shared a common bond and in Styal's history, they forged a milestone and a monument representing time and change.

Prior to Samuel Greg's visit in 1784, Styal was a small community of farmers who rented their land and thatched cottages from the wealthy land owner, Lord Stamford and Warrington of Dunham Massey. Although the pronunciation was the same, Styal up until that period, was spelled the old fashioned way and according to land deeds, as: Styall. In the parish district of Bollin cum Norcliffe and township of Pownal Fee, both neighbouring on the Wilmslow perimeter, the farmsteads survived like Styall on livestock and agriculture. Nothing worthy of historical value ever invaded the privacy of Styall apart from the foraging of Cavaliers and Roundheads during the civil war. If rumour can be relied on, it is said that Bonnie Prince Charlie and his followers spent some time at the Shipon at Styall whilst they watered their horses and quenched their thirst before heading towards Wilmslow. Styall's past history is best revealed by the other names which the village was known, 'Styhale', 'Stiale', 'Stihal'. All three titles, derived from an Anglo Saxon/Danish word meaning in simple language: 'place for pigs'. This explanation of Styall's past, gives credance to the claim of Styall being a thriving community when livestock sales were common and swine herding was the main industry. With the additional agricultural market and the five ale houses which are claimed to have existed at the height of the agricultural era, Styall was developed into a farming settlement. By the time Samuel Greg came to Styall, only two drinking houses remained. The Horse Shoe Inn which was close to the village Smithy, was the more popular on market days whilst the Old Ship Inn at the central point of the village was often more frequented because of its location. The track which led to Wilmslow divided the village green from the cattle auction site on the Oakwood Farm Estate. It was also on the site of the village green that the punishment stocks were situated, almost in the shadows of the stone village cross. The cross was moved by the Greg's to the junction of Holly Lane and Altrincham Road.

The evolution of Styal under the guidance of Samuel Greg is well known. Apart from putting Styal on the map, he brought the industrial revolution to the village and from that time on, Styal, relied and revolved around the Greg's Cotton Spinning Mill. Even today, history papers are still written on the subject of the 'The Greg's of Quarry Bank Mill'.

By the time Dr Rhodes made his visit to Styal in 1894 the village had developed into a bustling community with everything and everyone seeming to have connections with the Quarry Bank empire. It is not suprising that the doctor felt guilty of trespassing on private property. The Greg's had by this time, purchased the 570 acres of Styal Village which previously had been rented from Lord Stamford. Styal belonged to the Greg's as did the mill workers and the cottages they lived in. Even the fresh country air of the village seemed tainted with the aura of Greg superiority. What Samuel Greg had started as an entrepreneur, his son Robert Hyde , had continued with diligence and expertise. The third generation of the Greg family fortune at Styal was now in the hands of Edward Hyde Greg. The status of Mr Greg at the time of Dr Rhodes' visit was very much the same as his predecessors in that, he expected recognition as the 'country squire' or 'lord of the manor'. Following in the traditions of the family, Mr Greg served as a justice of the Peace on the Macclesfield Magistrates Court.

The approaching twentieth century marked a downward spiral for the large cotton mills of the North of England. The Quarry Bank Mill at

Styal was no exception, it too was going through an economic decline. Fortunately, the geographic location of Styal and the non-availability of any alternate employment, tied the mill workers to their jobs even at the expense of taking a cut in their wages. Many times in the past, Mr Greg had cried poverty and a ten per cent reduction had been accepted by the employees in preference to the suggested closure of Quarry Bank Mill. For reasons best known to Mr Edward Hyde Greg, he declined the obvious alternative of injecting money into the business but, at the same time, he was known to have withdrawn large capital sums for other ventures and land speculation.

The Doctor's historic journey to Styal almost 110 years after the famed Samuel Greg had made his mark, had an impact which was to change the course of village history. On that day, he set off from Handforth station in the direction of Styal, breathing in the fresh country air and languishing in nature's wonderland. Skirting round the Stanneylands estate and turning southwards, he journeyed through the Dean valley towards Wilmslow. At the junction of the two rivers, the Dean and the Bollin, known locally as Twinney's Brow, the bearded Doctor Rhodes turned again at right angles and climbed the steep hill in the direction of Styal village. Walking along the country road named Styal Road, and passing between the farming communities of Norcliffe and Oak Farm, he arrived at the junction of Sagars Road and Altrincham Road. After refreshment at the Ship Inn and an opportunity to fill his notebook with the knowledge he had gained during his observations, he set off again to Handforth station, bidding 'Good-day' to Mr Henshall and Mr Mottershead, two of the local residents.

This dedicated man of idealism took his dream and his mental store of Styal's peaceful and idyllic setting, back to Manchester and in his professional capacity as Chairman of the Chorlton Union Board of Guardians, gave his report at the fortnightly meeting. This historic meeting at which Doctor John Milson Rhodes gave his glowing report of Styal, was addressed to the twenty five committee members of the 'Guardians of the Poor' at their headquarters in the All Saint's district of Manchester. Doctor Rhodes, distinguished and impeccable in both manners and dress, looked considerably older than his 47 years. In a speech which was wrought with passion and fervour, he pleaded with his fellow Guardians to take notice of what he was about to tell them. Normally a shy man who avoided the limelight and carried the burdens of society on his shoulders, he now rose to the occasion with an undeniable enthusiasm. The Doctor's dilemma and the Guardians' concern, was to once and for all, rid the Manchester Withington Workhouse of it's child inhabitants. His mission to the peaceful Styal Village and his sojourn along the banks of the Dean was still fresh in his mind along with the inspiration he had encountered. After a long and carefully worded appeal, he outlined the advantages of taking the Workhouse children away from the pauper degradation and evil influences at Withington, to a place of beauty and an abundance of nature. After great discussion and contemplation, Mr Tomlinson seconded the motion which called for a committee to be set up to look into the possibility of removing the children of the overcrowded workhouse and transferring them to the Styal locality. The vote was carried by a two thirds majority and the 'Styal Option' became the codeword by which the elected sub-committee referred to in their proposals of purchasing the Styal Estate and the eventual building of a colony in which to house every child who was under the workhouse influence.

Emmeline Pankhurst, the better known of the Women's Rights Movement, also served as a Guardian of the Poor Law with the Chorlton Union in South Manchester. At the age of 36 years, and with a burning ambition to involve herself in the political scene, she befriended Mr Keir-Hardy of the Independent Labour Party. This juncture of her life coincided with her election to the Chorlton Board of Guardians. Together with Mrs Massey, she represented the Openshaw district of Manchester at her first meeting at Christmas time of 1894. Mrs Pankhurst, the fairly well to do wife of Dr Pankhurst - a barrister- came face to face with Doctor Rhodes at the Christmas meeting of new members. Each knew the other by reputation and a respect and understanding was forged from their first handshake. Whilst Dr Rhodes was a household name throughout Manchester, Mrs Pankhurst was making inroads on the political scene with her much publicised appearances at public meetings. Her success in having gained a seat on the Board of Guardians was her first rung on the political ladder of her future.

If Dr Rhodes needed an ally and a strong arm to carry out his ambitions plan for evacuating the workhouse children, he had found one in the form of Emmeline Pankhurst. It was no accident that found Mrs Pankhurst being placed on the sub-committee to proceed with the Styal option. Knowing of the reputation for hard work and self commitment to any task set before her, Dr Rhodes became more reassured by her presence. The many duties of the doctor as Chairman of the Chorlton Union and his work load at the Withington Workhouse hospital wing, made it impossible to commit himself whole-heartedly to his Styal project.

A 'pauper' by dictionary standards, is a person who is poor, destitute, poverty stricken, and supported by the public. In the words of general Booth of the Salvation Army the description is more vivid and to the point.

> " No Englishman can come upon the rates so long as he has anything whatever left to call his own. When long continued destitution has been carried on to the bitter end, when piece by piece every article of domestic furniture has been sold or pawned, when all efforts to procure employment have failed, and when you have nothing left except the clothes in which you stand, then you can present yourself before the relieving officer and secure your lodgings in the Workhouse."

Withington Workhouse, one of the largest in England, was the headquarters of the poor and needy who resided within the boundary of the Chorlton Union. The hospital accommodation which had been added to the main building over the years, was full to capacity with the sick, the infirm and the dying. At the time Mrs Pankhurst first visited the workhouse on official business, she was met with an experience which imprinted its self on her mind for years to come. Apart from an institution which was bursting at the seams with new born babies to old aged men and women, she came face to face with imbeciles, lunatics, epileptics and all manner of maimed and sick people. The population of the Chorlton Union which was increasing every year, reflected itself in the overcrowding in the casual and full time wards of the workhouse. Able bodied woman with no qualifications acted as nurses in the hospital and infirmary. Men, who were abled or disabled were required to work in order to satisfy the rules of the Workhouse Master and also to ensure their security of lodgings.

Emmeline Pankhurst, remembered vividly, the young seven year old girls and boys whom she saw scrubbing the vast corridors and work rooms. Such was the impact of those pale faced sparsely dressed children who contrasted so graphically with her own family, she left the Withington Workhouse on that day, with a determination to effect the removal of all children to the fresh country air and the sunshine of Styal.

In all fairness to the Chorlton Board of Guardians, they had tried to compel the Bishop of Manchester to take the workhouse children into the Poor Law Schools in Manchester and district during 1893. The Bishop's reply was to the effect that the task was too great and that he could see no future in pursuing the matter. This seemingly blunt refusal caused Dr Rhodes and his committee to seek out their own solution. This rejection by the Bishop caused Dr Rhodes to make his historic journey into the Styal hamlet.

Since the 1891 Government Act which made Free Education compulsory, the children of the workhouse obtained an elementary education under the guidance of a registered Poor Law teacher. The Withington Workhouse boys received a further training in such trades as shoe making, tailoring and gardening, whilst the girls had a compulsory training in all aspects of domestic duties and laundering. A Drill Instructor which was considered to be a neccessity in every workhouse or institution, also doubed as the Band Master. At Withington the band boys were prepared for Her Majesty's Regiments by the time they were thirteen.

Mr and Mrs Howell, the Master and Matron of Withington Workhouse, were pleased and proud of their achievements as far as the children were concerned. They cherished the fact that most children were placed into society in a trade where the majority were successful. Domestic servants were always heavily in demand and the Chorlton Guardians had a reputation for well mannered and obedient servants who were good hard workers. The same rule applied to the boys, who were apprenticed into all kinds of industry including the Manchester Boys Messenger Brigade.

By Custom and by government legislation, the Board of Guardians of each Union throughout England were obliged to off load as may children as possible in order to lighten the burden of the ratepayers, also keeping to a minimum the expenditure on workhouse inmates. Almost by invitation, the government licenced raiding parties made their annual descent on the Withington workhouse just as they had done last year and the preceeding fifteen or so year's before. The Manchester and Salford Refuges Society which was formed to rescue the so-called 'street arabs' and 'street urchins' of the Manchester slums during the Charles Dickens era, had maintained a good record of success under the leadership of Leonard K Shaw, one of the founders of the Manchester ragged Schools. The momentous task in providing security and hope to thousands of children who faced a life with no future, incorporated the well tried principle of Doctor Barnardo. The continuous flow of waifs and strays through his home was only viable so long as the rear exit door was kept open. In this same context, the exit from the Manchester Strangeways Home, was down the well trodden road or railway line to Liverpool, where Mrs Birt's Children's Rescue Home, doubled as a staging post before transportation to the dominion of Canada.

For the past twenty or so years, Canada had served as a dumping ground for thousands of English children, many of whom were orphans. Others included Workhouse children and those with relatives who somehow found themselves caught up in the net of the child export trade. Whilst the ratepayers and the philanthropical societies had benefited from the reduction in their burdens of charge, the Canadian homestead farmers of Ontario were able to survive and prosper with the help of the inexpensive child labour which was so freely exported from the mother country. In this atmosphere of the 1893 period, it is easy to see why the well trained workhouse children were singled out as being prime export fodder. After the Manchester Refuges, next in line were the Mill owners and the Military Band masters. Another source so far as the boys were concerned, was the Grimsby Trawlermens Association, who, each year, put in their request for able bodied boys to serve as apprentices on the fishing trawlers.

WITHINGTON WORKHOUSE AND INFIRMARY – MANCHESTER 1900

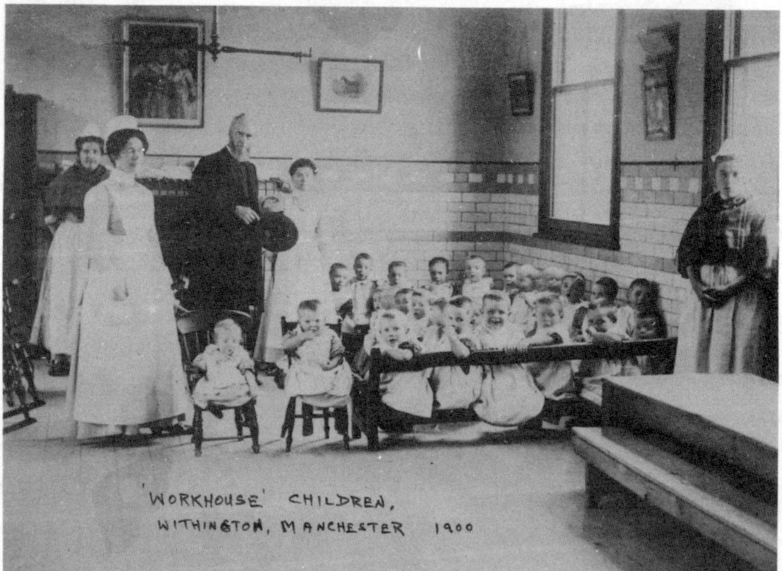

'WORKHOUSE' CHILDREN,
WITHINGTON, MANCHESTER 1900

Chapter 2

THE PAUPERS DISCIPLES

It has been said of Dr Rhodes:-

"No man has done so much to improve on the Poor Law in the last quarter of a century than John Milson Rhodes. He was a disciple to the poor and suffering and brought about many new changes."

Throughout Britain, Europe and America, Dr Rhodes had been paid many tributes, but just one sentence in a commemoration to him summed up his achievements and did justice to a great man:

" What Dickens started in fiction, John Milson Rhodes started in fact."

Amidst the background of middle class family life, John Milson Rhodes began life in a suburb area of Salford, called Broughton, in ~~during the year~~ 1847. Following his brother's footsteps, he progressed from Owens College in Manchester to become a medical student in Glasgow and Edinburgh. After another period of study at the Manchester School of Medicine and further studies at Brussels, he emerged with the necessary qualifications to start his own medical practice. Almost immediately after obtaining his degree, he started as a Family Practioner in the well-to-do district of Didsbury, a suburb of South Manchester. Little is known of the early life of the tall and eligible shy young bachelor during a period when seemingly, he had reached the top of the ladder and all indications pointed to a comfortable and succesful future.

If Dr Rhodes settled in Didsbury by chance, it is reasonable to assume that fate dictated his career from that moment on. His future was spelled out to him after his first visit to the Hospital in the neighbouring district of Withington. It happened on a day in 1872 when his carriage brought him to the gates of the Withington Workhouse and Infirmary. Although the buildings were only fifteen years old, the solid structure of the victorian architecture gave the impression of an endless age of deep rooted institutionalism. The sprawling complex of the buildings, doors and gates which emerged from the Nell Lane entrance, gave a claustrophobic feeling of confinement. His mission that day was to attend patients who were bedridden in the so called Infirmary Pavillions. Mrs Fanny Howell, the Workhouse Matron, accompanied him as he made a tour of the pavillions. The Matron was quite proud of the newly built hospital wings which had been added on the workhouse and she took great delight in telling the Doctor that the famous Florence Nightingale had given encouragement and help in the design of the hospital section of the workhouse. Impressed as he was, the young doctor could not take his mind off the sights and sounds which befronted him at every opening and closing of the doors within the institution. The seeds of Dr Rhodes' future were sown the very moment the tall iron gates of the workhouse closed behind him. Such was the impact and the memories of the workhouse teeming with human degradation and suffering, he made a promise to himself to devote his spare time to the cause of the workhouse inmates. The relationship between the doctor and the workhouse climaxed in the year 1878 when, at the expense of his practice at Didsbury, he agreed to join the Chorlton Union as the Overseer of the Union and the Withington Workhouse.

From the time of accepting the all important position as Overseer, the fate of Dr Rhodes and the workhouse became signed and sealed. his commitment and unselfishness in relieving the men, women and children of the South Manchester Workhouse, would secure his complete devotion until the end of his life. Amongst the many accomplishments at the largest workhouse in Manchester, he was responsible for the first trained nurses to be enrolled in the workhouse. Prior to that time, the nursing had been entrusted to the women inmates of the institution. Under his guidance, the Northern Workhouse Nursing Association was formed, with its policy of employing and recruiting skilled nurses. Apart from Styal and his cause for the workhouse children, his distinction lay in the relatively unknown field of Epilepsy. His search for a cure for this type of illness, took him to America and Europe and he also wrote a thesis on the subject which was published in three languages. As a man of medicine, his greatest moment came in 1904 when, in recognition of his devout services to the cause of Epilepsy, he was requested to lay the foundation stone at the Chorlton Union's new colony for Epileptics, at Langho in Lancashire.

The Overseer of the late nineteenth century who was answerable to a

Committee of Guardians and the Local government Board Inspector, was a far cry from the first overseer of the 16th century. A decree in the year 1572 gave an official licence and authority to the Parish Overseers throughout the country. The title of 'Overseer of the Poor', was in fact the first change to the Poor Law charter which had been in existence since the year 1010. At that time in history, a law was passed which commited one third of church tithes to the relief of the poor. Nearly six hundred years elapsed before a major amendment to the existing Poor Law was made. Known as the 'First Official Poor Rate', the Overseer was required by law in 1597 to levy a rate on every householder in his parish, for the purpose of assisting the poor. Within a short space of four years, another amendment known as 'The Great Poor Law' was put into effect in the year 1601 by Sir Thomas Egerton. This new act, specified in particular that Overseers were to be elected by parishoners of substance and ability. Also included in the 'Great Poor Law' was the right for employers to take on the services of child apprentices from the age of seven years. Another appendage to this act was to make punishable the offence of being; 'idle poor', 'beggar', 'rogue' and 'vagabond'. The continuing chronology of the Overseers became highlighted again in 1723 when the famed 'Workhouse Act' became law. Regarded as a milestone, the Overseers of the Poor Law were now empowered to provide Poor Houses with a Workhouse Annexe. In 1802, the Overeers were given the task of enforcuing the new law which limited the working hours of children to no more than twelve a day.

Probably regarded as the greatest breakthrough to date, was the so called 'New Poor Law' of 1834. Under this new legislation, children of the factories and other places of work, were required by law to receive education for up to six hours per day. Such was the abuse of the Workhouse Act of 1723, it was no surprise when government legislation brought in new laws to control the small Parish Workhouses which had mushroomed in the industrial areas of England at an alarming rate. Sometime within the 1837/8 period, a new image took shape amongst the many Poorhouses and Workhouses. The restructure of the Workhouse system brought a new concept and produced a new expression known as the 'Union'. The main purpose of the Union, was to amalagmate all the small parishes into one central township and all the villages and districts into one main regional district. At this point in time when centralised control became more popular, the beginnings of the Chorlton Union emerged, embracing with it all the districts of Manchester to the southern perimeter. The elected representatives of each district formed themselves into a governing body and were subsequently known as 'Guardians of the Poor' or, 'Board of Guardians'. Amongst the many amendments to the Poor Law came the much disputed 1847 Act, which not only wiped out all the small Poorhouses come Workhouses but also set new standards in the future of Workhouse institutions. Very simply, the new 'One Workhouse - One Union' law, spelled out the beginning of the large victorian institutions which, under one roof, housed all manner of human suffering. The inmates of the Workhouse were divided and separated into different categories which also meant that wives were separated from husbands under the strict laws of the Workhouse. The classification of workhouse inmates ranged from; the aged, the impotent and the children to the able bodied males and able bodied females. All children and able bodied females were required to do Oakum picking and firewood chopping whilst all able bodied men were given the task of stone breaking. The aged and impotent poor were comprised of a very mixed bunch of ailing people. Not least were the aged and infirm. The other helpless beings consisted of blind persons, lame and maimed persons, chronically sick persons and epileptic and lunatic persons.

By the time Dr Rhodes was awarded the Chairmanship of the Chorlton Union Board of Guardians in 1894, the Withington Workhouse had multiplied ten times over. Bursting at the seams with the continuous tide of incoming poor and destitute, the situation was forever at crisis point for more space. It was already obvious that children should not be a part of a lifestyle which condemned them to bear the stigma attached to pauperism and institutionalism. By removing the children to a place more suited to their welfare, the Doctor was also creating the space he needed in the over crowded Workhouse where the queue for accommodation was never ending. First and foremost however, the foothold which had been gained at Styal, was still in the balance and at a critical stage of negotiation. Many were the bridges and obstructions yet to be crossed before the Workhouse children were to catch a glimpse of the Cheshire sunshine. Just as sure as fate had brought Dr Rhodes to Didsbury and Withington, fate was about to introduce another person of destiny who, as yet, was a complete stranger to the world of the Workhouse and even more of a stranger to John Milson Rhodes, the man with a mission.

In 1894, a poll was held to elect a new member for the Openshaw district of Manchester, to represent them on the Chorlton Union Board of Guardians. The successful candidate, with an overwhelming majority, was a woman. Her name, as it appeared on the Polling Notice, was; **Emmeline Pankhurst,** (Married Woman).

'Oakum Picking' in the Workhouse. c.1895.

MRS. PANKHURST.

(From a Photograph by W. H. Warburton, Harris Promenade, Douglas, Isle of Man.)

Chapter 3

1894

Manchester and it's rainfall, is a time worn music hall joke which persists to the present day. The year 1894 was no wetter and no drier than normal, but in some respects it was a year of great significance to the Chorlton Union Board of Guardians. In a leading article, the Manchester Weekly Times christened 1894 as 'The Year of the Water'. It was perfectly true that an abundance of water had descended on Manchester during the year but not, from the heavens. Historically speaking, the reasons which prompted the title referred to the three major events of the year, each one connected or appertaining to water. Firstly, the Manchester Ship Canal having just been opened, was expected to be the bearer of future prosperity to the city of Manchester. Secondly, because of an increased water supply to the city, hydraulic power became popular and was made available for public use. Last but by no means least, the water from the illimitable resources of Lake Thirlmere in the Lake District, came on tap to the general public.

So far as the Chorlton Board of Guardians were concerned, the year of 1894 became a milestone in their objective of procuring a future for the Workhouse children. Dr Rhodes initiated the first move by advertising in various newspapers for 'people with land for sale, to reply in the first instance'. The emphasis was made in particular to those with land in a country environment. The overwhelming number of replies was finally reduced to just three. A plot of land at both Withington and Stretford were given consideration before that Spring day finally arrived when he discovered the alternative choice of Styal. In the Doctor's mind, nothing could compare with the Styal option and in pursuing this aim, he was unaware of the chain reaction or the events which were about to follow.

By coincidence, the land which the Guardians were pursuing at Styal had previously been sold in 1865, the same year in which the Withington Workhouse was completed. Lord Stamford and Warrington who was known as 'George Harry' to his friends, had offered the land to Mr Greg who, twelve months earlier, had purchased the adjoining 565 acres of Styal village. However, since Edward Hyde Greg would not meet the asking price, an auction was arranged. As a result of the sale, the Oak Farm Estate which faced the Greg estate on the opposite side of Styal Road became the property of Mr John Lawrence Lambe. In what was to be seen as a strange similarity of circumstances, Mr Greg, in 1894 having heard rumours of outside interest in the Oak Farm Estate, made an approach to Mr Lambe to secure the land for himself. The valuation of the estate in Mr Greg's eyes, fell far short of Mr Lambe's asking price and since no agreement could be reached, the land was offered to Dr Rhodes who was the Chief Negotiator as well as the Chairman of the Chorlton Union Board of Guardians.

The older generation of Styal who still reside in the village, are familiar with an old story which is purported to be true. It is claimed that Mr Edward Hyde Greg of Quarry Bank, who was in attendence at the auction of the Oak Farm estate along with Dr Rhodes and other interested parties, nodded off at the precise moment of bidding and awoke to realise his foolish error. It is also said that in his anger over the loss of the land, he planted a row of Poplar trees along the perimeter of his Norcliffe farm Estate in order to blot out his folly and, the view of the new aquisition of the Chorlton Guardians. The facts which refer to the barrier of Poplar trees are true although it took another two years before the actual deed. Contrary to the well known legend of the land sale of 1894, the story which is a myth, can be disproved and laid to rest. Sufficient factual and conclusive evidence is available which points to the private agreement between Dr Rhodes and Mr Lambe in a conveyancing which did not necessitate a public auction.

And so it had finally happened. In a year which began with the first ocean liner ploughing a future of hope and prosperity down the new seaway into Manchester, Dr Rhodes applied his signiture to a piece of paper which would change the lives of the children of the Workhouse. It did not happen overnight nor over a few weeks. From the time of Dr Rhodes foray into Styal during the Easter period, and after many weeks of proposals and counter proposals, six long months went by before the final agreement was reached. On the 21st of September 1894, the Chorlton Union of South Manchester along with the necessary backing of the Local Government Board, agreed terms with the Styal Landowner. Another two nail biting months passed before the legal documents came forward for the final signatures of both parties. November the 27th, 1894, became the day when the

Chorlton Board of Guardians by Law, became the legal landowners of the vast acreage of Styal. Dr Rhodes and his Clerk, Mr Bloomfield, breathed a sigh of relief as they signed the all important document. This moment was the climax to the long and hard fought battle to gainafoothold in the Cheshire country garden called Styal.

The vendor of the Styal Estate, Mr John Lawrence Lambe, was a businessman who traded in the cities of Manchester and London. All that is known of Mr Lambe, is that the legal deeds show his place of residence as; 63 St James Street, London, and 'Broomhurst', Dorking Surrey. The hub of the real estate which now belonged to the Guardians was the Oak Farm with its Shipon and Cottage. The tenant of the farm was Mr Gradwell, who farmed most of the land from Styal Road down to the Dean Valley. Since there was already an Oak Farm on Mr Greg's estate, the Oak Farm which now belonged to the Chorlton Guardians,was to become known as 'Oakwood Farm'. Half a mile down the Styal Road to the village junction, a small cluster of cottages and a Smithy, formed the Sagars Road boundary. The encircling perimeter meandered on to the wooded Dean Valley, taking in the Highfield House - now the Guardians property - then doubling back along the boundary of Lacey Green to the Wilmslow border of Bollin-cum-Norcliffe, Pownall, Carrs Wood and the steep hill known as Twinneys Brow. It had not been the intention of the Guardians to become land owners or property speculators but since Mr Lambe would not divide the estate, the alternative was to purchase the whole 300 acre estate. Amongst the first cottage tenants of the Chorlton Guardians and whose lives were to change dramatically over the next few years,were; Messers. Mottershead, Worthington, Walton, Morrsion, Henshall and Miss Shaw. On the advice of the Local Government Board, an application was made to the prosperous corporation of the City of Liverpool to borrow £20,000 required to pay Mr Lambe. As expected, the Liverpool Coporation duly complied with the Chorlton Guardians wishes and the formal agreement was drawn up for Dr Rhodes signature. In the agreement, the Chorlton Guardians agreed to repay Liverpool Corporation over a thirty year period, by annual installments of principle and subject to three and a quarter per cent interest.

Whilst on paper the aquisition of the Styal Estate appeared to have gone smoothly and according to plan, the Guardians were under no illusion about their material gain being the bottom rung of a very rickety ladder. The next all important phase before any further progress could be made, would be the planning permission application. In this respect, the head on collision with Mr Greg and the Wilmslow District Council was unavoidable and the application was seen as a direct challenge. Already, the Chorlton Guardians had felt the wrath of the powerful and influential individuals of Styal and Wilmslow and they considered the encounter a foretaste of what was yet to come.

The battle for the Styal option had begun in September when Dr Rhodes and Mr Lambe had both given a firm handshake on their agreement. In retrospect, that handshake had been tantamount to throwing down the gauntlet to the infuriated Mr Edward Hyde Greg, the master of Styal. As soon as Mr Greg became aware of the intentions of Dr Rhodes and the Chorlton Guardians, he immediately instigated a plan of opposition. In what Mr Greg termed as the 'Pauper invasion on Styal's doorstep' and 'Manchester's Workhouse overspill into Cheshire's countryside', he personally headed a petition which included an alliance of the Greg families, the many servants and friends of Mr Greg of Quarry bank, and lastly, the all powerful lobby of Wilmslow councillors and the friends and aquaintances of Mr Greg. Even the local newspaper known as 'The Advertiser' showed support for Mr Greg in it's first article on the subject, entitled; 'Cottage Homes for Pauper children' "It seems as if Styal is to be blessed with a Cottage Home. The local Goverment Board have complied with the request of the Chorlton Board of Guardians that they should be allowed to purchase a site at Styal for such a home. Of course one can understand the feelings of those who petitioned against the movement, and I think the Chorlton Board of Guardians might have found a suitable site in their own district instead of fastening upon Styal".

Mr Greg's petition was not successful and for the moment his next move was to work out a strategy for overcoming the necessary planning permission. The protestations and much quoted abuse aimed at the Chorlton Guardians, descended on Styal and Wilmslow to take root and fester. Such was the ill feeling which Edward Hyde Greg had created throughout the district. Even before one brick had been laid or one cottage erected, and even before the arrival of a Manchester workhouse orphan, the innocent children of Withington Workhouse had been condemned as social outcasts. Rumours were rife in the Styal neighbourhood where the already stigmatised pauper children of the Workhouse became aberrations of deseased children, street urchins, pick pockets, theives, criminals, imbeciles and what ever else that could be conjured from a Charles Dickens novel.

Another article in the Wilmslow Advertiser in 1894, mentioned the Local Government Board's letter which approved the Chorlton Guardians proposals to build cottage homes for Workhouse children at Styal. Mr Tomilinson, one of the Guardians,was quoted as saying: "the Board had been on tenterhooks for some time but were now able to congratulate themselves. Also, the petition of certain of the inhabitants of Styal and Wilmslow who had spoken of the new homes as a Pauper Colony, had not had the desired effect. He firmly believed that in the course of time, the gentlemen who had opposed the scheme, would be the first to come forward and assist in making the life of the children, brighter and happier ".

Why Mr Greg branded the Workhouse children as untouchable is unexplicable in view of his own family background. Both his father and grandfather had welcomed the workhouse children as useful labour at Quarry Bank Mill. Even in his own childhood, Mr Greg had witnessed the Styal Mill apprentices. Could it be that the return of Workhouse Paupers to Styal shared too many similarities and coincidences of the Greg empire of days gone by. History tells us that the Workhouse children employed by the Greg's were well looked after, even if they were worked to death. In all probability, the return of workhouse children to Styal would be a constant reminder to Mr Greg of his own family involvement with the very same children now condemned by his own words.

1894 and it's saga of event's, ended with a last ditch effort by Mr Greg by way of a carefully worded letter to the Chorlton Board of Guardians. Whilst the true stature of his authority showed through his words of criticism, the letter ended on a strangely out of character tone of humbleness. In a report of the Chorlton Guardians committee meeting, the Manchester City News recorded the following paragraph:-

"At a meeting of the Guardians of the Chorlton Union, a letter received from Mr E H Greg of Quarry Bank, Styal, was read out to the members by Dr Rhodes. The letter which related to the proposed Union Schools at Styal, went on :-

'If these schools were erected as proposed, my choice sites for first class villa residences would be ruined, as would also some choice sites on the Board's land. Furthermore, if the schools were erected at the Styal end, they would not interfere much with my property. I regard the establishment for three hundred pauper children on a costly residential estate as a death blow to the privacy, the rusticity and the out of the worldliness, of the old fashioned hamlet of Styal – (interruption of laughter by the Guardians) and also the value of my land property there – ('Oh') – In conclusion, I hope the Guardians would not think I was meddling – (laughter again)."

It was decided to leave the letter on the table and no action was taken.

Chapter 4

SNOWFLAKE

As seen through the eyes of the country onlooker, 1895 was a year of little or no significance at Styal Village. The landscape remained intact, the changing seasons came and went, and apart from the occasional visit to the Oak Farm Estate by strangers and officials from Manchester, the year had passed in a relative country calmness. Yet, to the more enlightened residents of Styal the serenity of the district was superficial and akin to the stilled atmosphere before the storm. Change was in the air. Change was in the elements of nature. Change was in the cloud which had settled over the Styal Village, waiting for the right moment. The expectant diversity which had been born from rumour and speculation had not materialised. The conclusion therefore, was that 1896 would now be the expected year of change.

Whilst progress had appeared to be almost non–existent on the Styal Estate of the Chorlton Guardians, 1895 would qualify as a year of unbelievable achievement and a year of great progress on behalf of the workhouse children. The formation of what was to be known as the 'SBSC' – Styal Building Sub Committee, began it's operations almost from the word go. Although Dr Rhodes as Chairman presided over the meetings, it was now the overall responsibility of the newly formed SBSC to carry out proposals. Dr Rhodes had been assured by Mr Jenner Fust the local Government Board Inspector, that the necessary planning permission would or should be a formality and that the intentions of the Chorlton Guardians should not come up against any further obstacles. Apart from the Doctor and his Clerk Mr Bloomfield, the SBSC consisted of Messrs, Deakin, Tomlinson, Mainwaring, Pankhurst, Halliday and Jennison. The eight members of the Styal Sub–Committee were resolute in their objective so far as the Styal option was concerned, but because of the social and political rivalry between the Guardians in general, friction would give cause for concern at frequent intervals. Two of the most volatile commitee members who often clashed in a verbal war of abuse, built up such a hatred of each other that they had to be kept apart. The two culprits were; Mr Harry Hilditch Mainwaring, a Boot Manufacturer of Hulme, Manchester and Mrs Emmeline Pankhurst, a housewife of 43 Buckingham Crescent, Victoria Park, Withington.

Mr Mainwaring, a long serving member of the Chorlton Guardians,was also a staunch conservative who carried the flag of male dominance to extremes, whilst Emmeline Pankhurst stood her ground as a newly elected Guardian and a new convert of Mr Keir Hardy's Independent Labour Party (ILP). Dr Rhodes, who refused to be involved in political agenda, was known to stand by Mrs Pankhurst on many issues and it was just a matter of time before they became good friends. Having been brought up in Salford and with a similar background, the Doctor and Mrs Pankhurst both found themselves sharing the same platform of everyday life. The bond which was forged from being close neighbours and working partners was to the advantage of Withington Workhouse and the under priveleged people in general.

In what can be termed as it's challenge, the SBSC were requested to scour the country and report back with their views on the various children's homes and the methods of each system. The second motion, was the all important planning and building of the Children's Colony at Styal. On this issue, the board were unanimous in their proposals to advertise publicly a competetion which would challenge architects to submit a plan of buildings and homes on the Styal Estate. A suggestion that the first three winning entries should receive a prize of £75, £50 and £30 respectively was approved.

On the fourth Friday in April 1895, the 25 Guardians of the Poor Law for the Chorlton Union of South Manchester, assembled in the oak panelled boardroom at the Union Headquarters. The hum of excitement on that day was unmistakable, and the atmosphere of the room was heavy with anticipation. On the day's agenda, one item stood out as being the reason behind the unusual interest which was under discussion even before the meeting commenced. The sentence read:- 'Styal - Cottage Homes and Schools Awards' The Manchester City News gave an accurate insight to the events of the meeting and the subsequent report went as follows:- 'Eighteen sets of designs were received for the Cottage Homes of Styal. Mr Anderson in the course of his awards stated: ' I have examined the designs in terms of merit in design and adaptability. I have no hesitation in placing the designs in the following order: (1) SNOWFLAKE, (2) A HOME, (3) Q.E.D It is however extremely unfortunate that the author of 'Snowflake' provides accomodation for 286 children only, instead of 300 as required in the rules. Under the cirumstances I am reluctantly compelled to disqualify the Snowflake entry, and accordingly award the first prize to 'A Home' and the second prize to the author of the motto 'Q.E.D.' The third prize was awarded to the author of 'Sunshine Home'. Accordingly Messrs Charles Clegg & Co, King Street, Manchester, won £75. Mr J W Beaumont, St James Square, Manchester, £50, and Messrs W Telford Gunson and Son, Marsden Street, Manchester £25.

'The Guardians in consideration of the excellent report of the assessor upon the 'Snowflake' plans, have decided to adopt these, the author being Mr J W Broadbent of 1 Princess Street Manchester, and he has been entrusted with the carrying out of the work'

Incredibly, Mr Broadbent and 'Snowflake', with the distinction of being both winner and loser in the competition, came away from the meeting with the Styal contract firmly in his grasp.

Now that the issue concerning 'Snowflake' had been settled, the long awaited report and comments on the next phase was highlighted by several newspaper reports. The following article under the heading 'Cottage Homes for Pauper Children' was recorded thus: ' Dr Rhodes presiding, Mr Bloomfield read the report to be provided for the children chargeable to the Union, on the site recently acquired at Styal. With the object of obtaining a full knowledge of the details of the system of Cottage Homes, and the class of buildings amongst the most modern erections of the kind, the committee said they had personally visited and inspected the Poor Law Schools at Leicester, Hornchurch, Banstead, Swansea, West Derby, The Harris Institute at Preston and the Homes for Little Girls provided by Dr Barnado at Ilford, whilst a visit was paid by two members of the sub committe to the homes provided by the Countess of Meath, and also the School of Handicrafts for Boys. The committee were of the opinion that it was desireable to provide accomodation for rather more than the number of children now chargeable. Excluding 101 Roman Catholics now sent to certified Poor Law Schools, there are at the present time in the Workhouse, 275 boys, girls and infants. This is a normal number. The population of the Union is increasing rapidly, and pauperism holds pace. The committee recommended – (1) That plain substantial cottage homes, constructed to contain not more that 20 children, be erected on a site selected near Twinneys Bridge, on the land purchased for the purpose; (2) that provision be made for 120 boys and 160 girls and infants, (14 homes); (3) that a mixed school for the younger children be provided, and that arrangements be made to send the elder children to an outside school; (4) the erection of workshops and a bakehouse; (5) that wards for isolation be erected; (6) that provision be made for hospital accommodation; (7) the erection of an administrative block, (8) the provision of a swimming bath.

Some of the news items which did not make headlines during 1895 are now quoted to illustrate the workings of the Guardians and also to give an insight to the various subjects under discussion at the weekly meetings;

January: A lady sent a letter to the Guardians asking if they had any healthy young girls of good character at the workhouse,whom they would like to send to Canada with a party of other emigrants. The Guardians pointed out that the best girls were always selected for emigration to Canada. On this occasion, the board agreed that there was sufficient employment at home in their own surroundings for the girls who were eligible, and that the Canadian lady should be informed that no girls were available.

April: Mr Mainwaring was voted off Mrs Pankhurst's district to N0 5 district as it was impossible for them to work together.

May: The Prestwich Union who twelve months previous had suggested that a meeting be held between the three Manchester Unions to consider the formation of one Poor Law Union for the whole of Manchester, had recently approached the Manchester Union, with a request to dismember the Chorlton Union. The Union, (pop.300,000) opposed the move and voted against it.

June: Mrs Pankhurst suggested that the house standing on the land at Styal should be used as a temporary home for 25 children of Withington Workhouse who needed the immediate benefit of fresh air and sunshine.

June: The Board, after receiving continued complaints, held an inquiry into the supply of milk to the Workhouse. The findings once again proved evidence of dairy milk below the standard requirements – the milk having been watered down by as much as 18% – and it was decided to terminate the contract of the supplier and advertise for new tenders.

July: Allowed burial rights at Southern Cemetry at a cost to the Guardians of eight shillings under the age of ten years and fifteen shillings for persons ten years and over. The ministers fee of two shillings per burial service to be included.

August: Withington Workhouse boys are still in demand by Grimsby Skippers who are anxious that the Guardians should let them have any suitable lads when available. One boy now a man, has taken a wife and now owns his own trawler.

During November of 1895, the death occurred of one of Manchester's leading citizens Sir Charles Halle of Greenheys, Manchester, founder of the Halle Orchestra.

In the closing weeks of the year at a time when even the serious minded of the Guardians joined in the celebratory mood of achievement of the Styal project, it was obvious that the festive spirit was not unanimous. The atmosphere was somehow tinged with scepticism and cast a shadow of uncertainty. For some reason, the doubts and fears which had always been kept at arms length were beginning to breech the Guardian's wall of optimism. At a meeting at the end of November when the usual noisy and militant debate took place, one sentence was responsible for bringing the Guardians down to earth, and also back to reality. The minutes of that meeting which brought to an end the year of 'Snowflake' also showed in no uncertain manner the prospects of the year ahead.

November: 'Mr Deakin said it was scandalous that a Wilmslow man be given the contract for drainage at Styal when he was not a ratepayer of Manchester. 'Mr Deakin said the Ratepayers were going to have to subsidise the children at Styal Cottage Homes at one pound per head per week. 'Mr Apleton said: "These buildings would be a future white elephant".

Chapter 5

THE PRELUDE YEARS

'Work has begun on the land where the proposed new homes are to be erected by the Chorlton Guardians'. From this brief statement published in a Manchester newspaper of January 1896, one could assume that Guardians had settled their differences and had embarked on a firm based strategy for the year ahead. The board room at Grosvenor Square, All Saints, Manchester, could dispute this theory since the committee were still opposed on many issues on the subject of the Styal Cottage Homes. The ever reliable Manchester City News, portrays a concise diary of the year's events and is seen as a continuation of the unfolding saga of 'Snowflake'.

February: 'The Board of Guardians Committe felt that if the children could go to normal schools outside the gates of the new colony, then they would lose the pauper image.

After a mccting of thc managcr of the Wilmslow National Schools, it was decided not to accept any children from the workhouse because of the social implications. The Reverend Bates apologised to the Guardians and said if it had been up to him, it would have been different.'

'Wilmslow National Schools said the effect of Workhouse children on thc normal pupils would be of some consequence'.

February: 'The costs of the Styal Cottage Homes was highlighted at a noisy debate. The motion was carried by eleven votes to ten'.

May: 'Messrs. Mainwaring, Deakin, and Mrs Sale still opposed the Styal Homes and it's soaring costs and demanded government intervention. Dr Nolan argued that the boarding out system was the best and that after an exhausting inquiry, it was found that Styal Cottage Homes was not a practical experiment. He further said that : "On the Guardians decision that day, depended the lives and

happiness of hundreds and thousands of children."
Mr Mainwaring moved and suggested that the land at Styal could be utilised for the accomodation of imbeciles. Mr Deakin in seconding the motion, said that the Styal institution would be a serious death rate colony in consequence of the state of the River Bollin.'

'Messrs. Deakin, Mainwaring and Dean, were beaten by the vote in their bid to stop the Styal Cottage Homes scheme.'

July: 'A letter was received from the Wimslow District Council asking if the Chorlton Board of Guardians would consider allowing them to use the isolation hospital now being erected at Styal, in times of infection. Dr O Doherty said that Wilmslow should build an isolation hospital of their own, if so needed. Dr O Doherty also said: "When the Guardians wanted to get the children into the Wilmslow schools there, they would not allow 'pauper' children in. If they did not want anything to do with pauper children in their schools, it might even contaminate Wilmslow people to go into an infectious hospital, with so many pauper children about them. In order to keep up the respectability of the Wilmslow people, and that there should be no danger of contamination, the Guardians should not grant this request. Let them mind their own business".

August: 'At a meeting, it was reported that 3 children out of 144 sent to Canada from the Chorlton Union were troublesome, but the remainder appeared to be doing well. Mrs Sale proudly stated that only the hand picked children were chosen to go to Canada. The chairman Dr Rhodes reported: and we have to make do with all sorts'

'It was also reported that since 1892, forty four boys have been sent to the training ship 'Mercury' at Hamble, in Hants.'

November: 'An old boy from the Withington Workhouse wrote to the Guardians and mentioned the kindness of the Workhouse school master. He had been sent to Canada against his wishes but had now settled in Boston in the United States. Because of his band training, he was now playing for the best band in Boston'.

December: 'The Board offered condolences to Dr Rhodes on the death of his only brother, Dr T W Rhodes of Northenden'.

On a more positive approach to Styal, the Chorlton Guardians received a reply from Mr Balfour, Member of Parliament for Manchester East, that he would accept the invitation of the Guardians to lay the Cottage Homes foundation stone sometime during the year. Meanwhile, Mr Normanton, a Manchester builder, had won the Styal contract at a fixed price of £50,310 The skilled labour force was recruited from Wilmslow and Manchester with the Guardians insistent that the non-skilled labour should come from the men and boys of the Withington Workhouse.

Seemingly, the dust had settled on the sleepy pastureland of Styal. The sparring was now at an end and the opposing factions accepted their fate in a village which sighed a tranquil relief. The local village residents now observed with interest and speculation the building of the new colony, as yet unaware that their own future destiny was being shaped with every brick and every timber. Unfortunately, Mr Greg did not accept his defeat gracefully, for it was at this juncture during the laying of the foundations of the Cottage Homes, that with one last gesture of defiance aimed at the Guardians, he gave instructions to the tenant of his Norcliffe Farm Estate, to plant a row of sapling Poplar trees along the perimeter which faced the cottage colony.

In the history of Styal, August the 31st 1896, must rank as one of the most important dates on the village calendar records. The event which was reported in all the Manchester newspapers and the Wilmslow Advertiser, was the long awaited 'foundation stone laying ceremony'. Since Mr Balfour chose to use the occasion to emulate his views of the 'Poor Law', the whole day's events would take too long and involve a lot of unnecessary details so far as this story goes. The Wilmslow Advertiser chose to present a shortened and more compact record. Their report went as follows:- 'Cottage Homes at Styal'.

'On Monday Mr Balfour laid the Memorial Stone of the Workhouse Cottage Homes, which are being erected at Styal by the Guardians of the Chorlton Union, at a cost of over £50,000 for the purpose of bringing the children who are left in the Withington Workhouse, up in the country free from pauper influences. The weather was most unpropitious, a heavy rain falling throughout the proceedings. A large tent had been erected for the numerous people who had travelled from Manchester London Road Station by the noon train.

The officials included the Lord Mayor and Lady Mayor of Manchester, Dr Rhodes, all the committee of the Chorlton Board of Guardians, Chaplain T Horne and the Master of the Withington Workhouse, the Rector of Wilmslow, Rev E Bates and representatives of the Manchester and Prestwich Board of Guardians.

Mr Balfour arrived at Wilmslow Station at 1.20pm from Hawarden Castle and was driven to the site of the new homes.

After the introductions, Mr J B Broadbent the architect of the buildings, presented Mr Balfour with a handsome silver trowel, the workmanship of Messrs Elkington and Co. The blade of the trowel was very prettily mounted on it's shaft, with gold. The shaft was of ivory and was set with amethysts. The inscription on the blade was as follows: 'Presented to the Rt Hon Arthur James Balfour, First Lord of her Majesty's Treasury, on the occasion of his laying the foundation stone of the Cottage Homes and Schools at Styal, for the Guardians of the Chorlton Union. 31st August 1896. Dr Milson Rhodes MD Chairman. T Halliday, Chairman of Committee; D S Bloomfield, Clerk, Jas. B Broadbent, A.R.I.B.A. Architect.

The memorial stone bears the following inscription:- "This stone was laid by the Rt Hon A J Balfour, Member of Parliament for East Manchester, First Lord of Her Majesty's Treasury, 31st August 1896."

After the ceremony at Styal, Mr Balfour and all the Guardians and friends, were driven to Wilmslow and a luncheon of the most superb character was served at the Wilmslow Public Hall, the caterer being Mr Kenneth Gaskell of the Swan Hotel, Wilmslow.

Before all the dignitaries sat down to luncheon including Capt. Greg of Lode Hill Styal, the tables were photographed by Mr Rupert Stearn the well known photographer of Wilmslow.

Amongst the many letters of congratulations was one from Mrs Emmeline Pankhurst - a committee member - who, at the same time, expressed her deep regret at not being present as she was at Harwich. Mr McDougall of the Manchester Board of Guardians, said that all the Guardians in the country would watch the growth of the Styal Experiment with great interest.

Mr Balfour left Wilmslow Station during the evening and proceeded to Crewe, where he caught the Scots Express. The Rt. Hon. gentleman travelled direct to Whittingham where a house party was assembled. After a brief stay, he will then go to Balmoral for a week. Miss Balfour went North earlier in the day.'

All the boys of the Withington Workhouse who were engaged in the construction work of the new colony, were paraded by Mr Courbard, the workhouse bandmaster come drill instructor, for the day's ceremony. The rain had prevented the guard of honour duties which had been rehearsed and instead, the boys had to content themselves as background sentries and ushers. No one in the audience or the Village of Styal could have predicted the political outcome of Mr Balfour yet, everyone at the Cottage Homes ceremony that day was observing the future Prime Minister of England.

Towards the end of 1896, the Guardians having recovered from their setback in the search for school accomodation in Wilmslow, had by now unanimously decided to erect their own school on the site of the old cattle auction field, facing the Village Stocks. The Rev Bates of Wilmslow, was still apologising over past differences and had made an offer to take some of the children into existing schools in Wimslow providing that the Guardians paid for the necessary alterations. His suggestion was put to the local Government Board who flatly rejected the offer and refused to sanction £500 which was the sum needed to improve the school at Wilmslow. Unfortunately for the Rev Bates, the damage had been done and the Chorlton Guardians had decided on their own school which would accommodate

500 children. The last recorded chapter on this subject came at the April meeting of the Guardians in 1897:'It was decided to reject the offer of school accommodation at Water Lane, Wilmslow and the National Schools at Wilmslow, and that the school should be built on the estate'.

It was becoming apparent that the Styal Colony would not be finished on time and that another twelve months would be required to complete the project. Mr Tomlinson, a leading figure on the Board of Guardians was elected Chairman of the Board for 1897. However, an amendment brought by Mrs Pankhurst, suggested that Dr Rhodes should be re-elected as Chairman in order that he may be witness to the end product for which he had strived and that he may claim the just rewards for his commitment to the Styal Cottage Homes. Dr Rhodes was elected by 12 votes to 6 and Mr Tomlinson was elected as Vice Chairman.

'Mr J T Exton of the Grimsby Board of Guardians sent an urgent letter of appeal to the Chorlton Guardians requesting that they send as many boys as possible from the Withington Workhouse for the Deep Sea Fishing Trawlers. They explained that they could not recruit local people and the Grimsby Workhouse had no boys old enough to go to sea.'

The frustration was evident as the Chorlton Guardians complied with the unwritten rules of the workhouse system which allowed the institutions to poach from each other in order to satisfy the Government and the rate payers. Boys of all ages who had been taught a trade and schooled to a promising standard, were plucked from the workhouse at a moment's notice, just as they were when the emigration authorities required surplus children to make up a full cargo for the Canadian Dominion. There was very little that Dr Rhodes or the Guardians could achieve in their efforts to keep the children at the school desk. A revelation at the November meeting of the Guardians proved beyond all doubt that the Withington Workhouse was literally bursting at the seams.

Conditions in the South Manchester Workhouse are portrayed in the minutes taken from a meeting in December 1897:

'Such is the overcrowding in the Chorlton Union's (the second largest in the country) Workhouse, children's school rooms are being taken over and converted into dormitories. The Oakum Picking Sheds will have to double as sleeping quarters for the casual in-mates. The Manchester Guardians are being asked to take the able bodied men into their infamous Test House at Tame Street, Ancoats.

For the Chorlton Guardians, the year ahead promised to be better than the one now coming to a close. The beckoning project presented a new dawning for the workhouse children and a new era for the Chorlton Union . All things considered, 1898 should turn out to be a year of fulfilment and certainly the most important year in the history of child welfare and the Chorlton Board of Guardians.

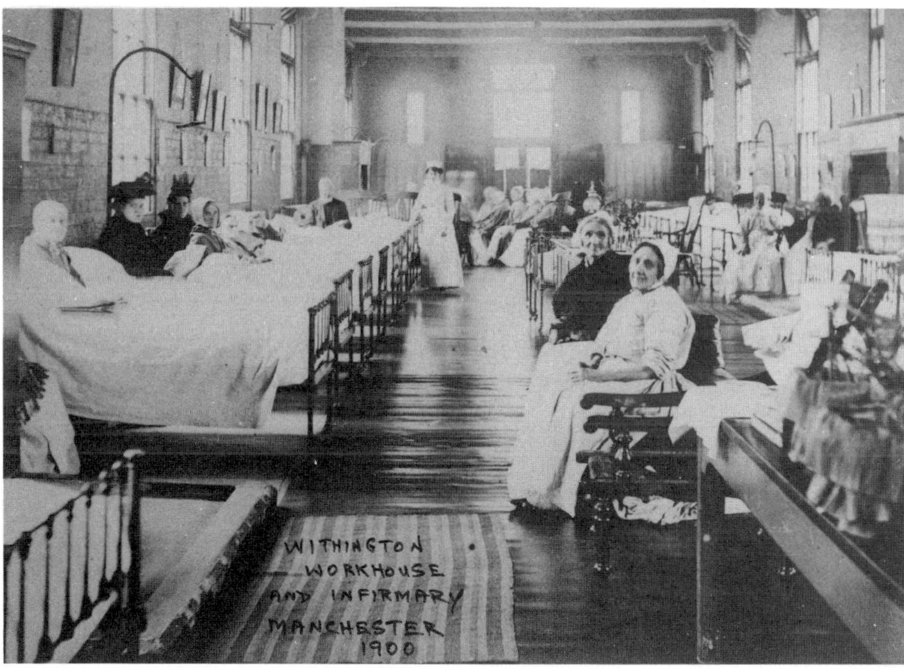

IN THE VILLAGE, STYAL

Styal Cottage Homes Entrance.

Chapter 6

THE EXODUS

'And it came to pass' - 'And so it was decreed'. Both these phrases are suggestive of a predestined fate and in a sense, 1898 proved to be just that. Indeed, the year of destiny had finally arrived for the children of the South Manchester Workhouse. The year not only belonged to the children but also to the Chorlton Board of Guardians and in particular to Doctor Rhodes and Mrs Pankhurst. Both stage and platform were in a state of readiness for the expected event of the year at Styal. Not since the early days of Samuel Greg's Mill at Quarry Bank, had the village seen such excitement and witnessed such hustle and bustle, the mild winter had given the necessary breathing space for the uninterrupted building of the colony and apart from any unforseen disaster, the contractors were now on course to reach their target by the summer time.

Back at the Guardian Offices at Manchester, the same enthusiasm had almost come to a standstill as the new year gave a nervous hiccup at the January agenda. Even at this late stage and only months away from the Styal finale, controversy still raged over the so called 'Styal Homes Venture'. The opponents of the scheme were full of criticisim over the soaring costs of the ratepayer's money on the Styal experiment and other venture. Mrs Pankhurst was singled out for squandering money on the low paid workers and criticised for campaigning for the relief of the poor. This particular meeting found Mrs Pankhurst engaged in a stand up battle in an argument concerning the pittance which was paid to the blind persons at Henshaw's Blind Asylum in Manchester. Somehow, the reference to Styal diminished during the early weeks of the year in favour of the tit for tat political rivalry which erupted with the usual fervour in the run in to the Local Guardian elections. One decision on the Styal venture which claimed the unanimous support of all the Guardians was the proposal that Mr Balfour - the leader of the House of Commons - should be asked to officially open the new Styal Cottage Homes, at a date to be arranged. By the time the April electioneering had got under way, rhetoric and verbal abuse came perilously close to personal accusation and libel. One such instance of local government and Board of Guardian election propaganda was the Chorlton Guardians meeting in April of 1898. At this meeting, the rate paying electors were asked not to vote for the Roman Catholics on religious grounds and not to vote for Ladies – the Conservatives having issued a bill saying: " sweep all the ladies off the Board of Guardians, luxury and extravagance is their policy".

Mrs Pankhurst survived the verbal onslaught as did most other guardians and the welcome pause for the Easter festivities brought about an uneasy but appreciative truce to all concerned. Perhaps the most important social event of the year in Manchester and the North West was the Easter offering of the famous circus ensemble of Barnum and Bailey. The Trafford Park venue boasted a huge canvas hippodrome which housed 14,000 people at one perfomance. Further afield, stories of Gold Strikes in the Canadian and Alaskan territories were making front page reading in most newspapers. At some time, it was reported that General Booth of the Salvation Army had recently departed to the North American continent to promote his work. In a farewell speech to England, he mentioned the 11,000 wretched men and women who sought shelter every night and the 18,000 starving men women and children who were given food every day. May 19th according to the newspapers brought the nation to its knees. It proclaimed the death of Mr Gladstone and the nation was made aware of the solemn importance of the occasion with newspaper editorial for weeks to come, all paying tribute to a once great Prime Minister.

Styal Homes was officially announced to the Manchester public at large in a special and exclusive report by a leading correspondent of a Manchester newspaper. In a pre-Easter edition, he accompanied Mr Broadbent the architect, Mr Bloomfield clerk, Mrs Pankhurst, Mr Tomlinson and other guardians on a tour of the Styal settlement.

"As we walked along the muddy lane from Handforth to the new settlement, breathing the sweet fine air that sweeps the Cheshire plain", thus wrote the reporter from the Manchester Weekly Times – "we arrived at a delightfully rural part of the country, about a mile from Handforth. The hedges and the trees were just putting forth the faintest signs of spring and all nature seemed awakening from it's winter sleep. First, we came to the school which is capable of seating 500 scholars and which will also double as a place of worship and a platform for concerts and meetings.

The school, which is situated about half a mile from the cottage colony was selected for weighty reasons, the board were anxious that the children shall go to school like other children, free from all suggestions that they are paupers. They hope that other children of the neighbourhood will enrol themselves on the books of the school. The board were looking forward to the day when the education authority of the district would take over the buildings and manage the establishment and accept the children of the cottage homes on the same conditions as the children of the village. Half a mile down the road, we arrived at the settlement which stands in an enclosure of fifty acres adjoining the River Dean, a tributary of the far famed Bollin. It was here that Mrs Pankhurst and Mr Tomlinson explained in detail the layout of the colony". After a very informative and informal day in the company of the guardians, the guest reporter concluded his write up with a chapter dedicated to the children ....

"The guardians of the Poor Law have many youngsters committed to their care, youngsters who came into the world with the most disadvantageous environment. At best they are the children of parents too poor to provide them with the necessities of life. It frequently happens that they are delicate and ill fed on their arrival, and others are born in the workhouse, or are deserted, and never know the authors of their being. The four methods of dealing with the children are:-

(Firstly) They may be retained in the workhouse school, where the taint of the workhouse is upon them all the time their little brains are developing. They become reconciled to the workhouse, the only home they know.
(Secondly) Another scheme for the treatment of pauper children is to take them away from the workhouse and mass them in some huge building, common to several unions. This is called the Barrack system, which may be found in operation in the Southern Counties. This has been condemned by the Local Government Board. Probably,it is worse than the workhouse school. Droves of children, lumped together, taught in huge batches by line and rule, have no opportunity of developing their separate individualities. They have an automatic training and when they come out into the world to fight life's battle, they find themselves with a serious disadvantage to the more quick witted experienced combatants.

(Thirdly) The next option is the Boarding Out System, which is in operation in many unions throughout the Kingdom. This is a plan which has much to commend it. A child is sent into the home of respectable people, is brought up to some extent as one of their own children, and is taught a trade under the guidance of its foster parents. The success of the system depends, of course, on the character of the home. The difficulty is the finding of homes of this description. Not every person cares to be responsible for the upbringing of a strange child drawn from a workhouse. On the other hand, there are many disreputable people who would jump at the chance of taking charge of a child who could drudge and slave for them from early morning until late at night, in return for the bare means of a living. Of course, the Guardians could not tolerate the sending of children into homes of this description, and the boarding out system has not solved the problem. The demand for children in suitable homes is not able to meet the supply.
(Fourthly) The establishment of the Cottage Homes System, in the opinion of the experienced members of the board, provides the most satisfactory solution. The Guardians, though absolutely convinced of the wisdom of building cottage homes, would not have sanctioned this large expenditure, in all probability, if their existing accommodation at Withington were capable of providing for the children. But it is not. Withington Workhouse at present, is in a terribly overcrowded condition. It was absolutely necessary to remove some of the inmates elsewhere, and it was, and is, felt that the best class to remove are the children. Even after they have gone, the workhouse will be tried to it's utmost capacity."

On a day when the Chorlton Guardians were engrossed in their affairs of the Poor Law, and at a time when decisions concerning the children hung in the balance, the letter from Styal arrived at the Guardian's headquarters. It was now, almost the end of May with summer almost on the doorstep. The important news from Styal was the completion date of the new homes which was given for September. The letter which pointed out in no uncertain manner, a colony of children without as yet a staff to run the institution, had the desired effect and the Guardians, realising the time factor and the urgency of the situation, instituted a plan of action. That very week, an advertisement was placed in all major leading newspapers for the posts of Headmaster at the Styal Homes School, and a Superintendent of the Cottage Homes. Within two weeks from the time of advertising, the Chorlton Guardians received no less than 650 applications for the position of Superintendent and 300 for post of Headmaster.

With the realisation that they were now committed and that the point of no return had been passed, the guardians adopted a business like approach to the Styal Homes. Every meeting brought Styal to the forefront, with proposals, counter proposals, amendments, new rules and regulations and a policy which would spell out a new concept for future child welfare. All in all, the weeks leading up to the summer holiday season proved to be a hectic time for the Styal sub committee and the two week holiday period provided a timely interlude before the oncoming opening ceremony of the new colony. Mrs Pankhurst chose this moment as in previous years, to travel to Geneva where her daughter was deposited with friends of the family for the summer vacation. This annual trek to Switzerland was the reason behind Emmeline Pankhurst's absenteeism at the foundation stone laying ceremony two years earlier. However, she made a promise to herself to be present at the forthcoming opening ceremony of the Styal Cottage Homes at any price. Fate and Emmeline Pankhurst seemed to walk hand in hand. Within days of her 40th birthday, she received an urgent telegram from her husband at Withington, begging her to return home to be with him, due to ill health. She responded with an immediate departure but her efforts were to no avail. On the last leg of the journey from London to Manchester, a train passenger who was engrossed in a late newspaper edition was unnaware that he had inadvertently exposed the headline news proclaimimg the death of ·Dr Pankhurst. At the Friday meeting of the Chorlton guardians on July 8th, Mr Tomlinson expressed his and the board's concern over the calamity which had fallen on Mrs Pankhurst. The death of her husband had been a tradgedy for Mrs Pankhurst who was a highly acquired member of the Guardians.

On the subject of the Styal Cottage Homes, the latest news from the committee was the recent communication received from the Rt. Hon. Mr Balfour. With apologies, he regretted that in all probability, and owing to the state of his health and the many pressing engagements, he would be unable to perform the opening ceremony at Styal. The committee decided to request the services of the Marquis of Lorne for the ceremony and in the event of his unavailability, Dr Rhodes should be called upon, to declare the schools open. In response to the Chorlton Guardians, the Marquis gave his consent to come down to open the Styal Homes. "He was afraid, that Princess Louise would not be able to accompany him and could fix no date earlier than September". As a result of a sub- committee being formed to inspect all applications for the post of Superintendent of the new homes, the following announcement was made:

"Mr William Shaw, master of the Chorlton Union Schools at Withington was duly elected Superintendent of the Union Cottage Homes, recently erected at Styal". This decision was made known at the Friday meeting of the Guardians on August 8th. "Mr Shaw, who was chosen from the final 479 applicants, was a pupil teacher at the Grosvenor Sq. schools in Manchester from 1873-8. He was then appointed to assistant master at St George's School, Altrincham until 1881. Since then he has been in the service of the Chorlton Union. With his appointment, which includes a furnished house plus light and ration, he will receive a salary of £150 per year."

On September the 1st, 1898, a Manchester leading newspaper recorded the sad news which the Chorlton Guardians had half expected. Never the less it was a bitter blow to Dr Rhodes and the members of the board when the announcement was made. 'Resignation of Mrs Pankhurst' "Mrs Pankhurst has resigned her seat as a member of the Chorlton Board of Guardians. In removing children from the far from suitable surroundings of the workhouse, Mrs Pankhurst displayed great interest and busied herself in the arrangements of the Styal Cottage Homes, where the little ones will be far more comfortably housed than they have hitherto been, and will further have less of the stamp of the pauper upon them. These homes will be opened on the 4th or 5th October 1898"

Many were the newspaper reporters who flocked to Styal on the 4th October 1898. It was the most significant day of the year to the Boards of Guardians throughout the country and the events of the day would be narrated in varying degrees, according to the Columnists point of view. Perhaps it was only natural that because of local interest, the 'Advertiser' of Wilmlsow were outstanding in their observations and almost a whole page was taken to describe with great accuracy, the day's events from start to finish. The following extracts from the Advertiser will give an insight to the events and atmosphere of the day:-

"On Tuesday afternoon a scheme which will be watched with the greatest possible interest by those having in hand the administration of the Poor Law, so far as it affects the bringing up of pauper children, was successfully floated, in the opening of the new cottage homes and school which have been erected at the pretty Cheshire village of Styal, near Wilmslow, by the Chorlton Union Board of Guardians.

The cottages and other buildings have been erected on the latest principles and are models of what such dwellings should be. The cottages for the girls include accommodation for a foster mother whilst the boy's homes will cater for a married couple who will act as foster parents, the father doubling as a technical instructor to the boys. The 308 children will be distributed in 16 homes which incorporates a probation Lodge home where newcomers will undergo a two week quarantine period thus preventing any spread of infectious disease. Great care has been exercised in the selection of suitable persons who will combine genuine kindness with the necessary firmness and discipline. The whole forms quite a little colony, or as it has been called, 'a children's village'. the boys and girls – the latter of whom will be brought up for positions in domestic service – will of course be kept apart in the actual occupation of the cottages, but otherwise, in daily life, they will be as brothers and sisters.

The good people of Didsbury were bitterly disappointed on Monday by the posting of two telegrams from Kensington Place to Dr Rhodes, of which the following are copies:–"Kensington Palace, Sunday. Bad cold and lost voice, make journey tomorrow unlikely of accomplishment. Will wire again". In reply to this, which was sent to Ivy Lodge, the residence of the worthy doctor, by special messenger, Dr Rhodes wired expressing his regrets on the threatened probabilities, and the cause that led up to them, but still hoping that the people of Didsbury would have the pleasure of according his lordship a hearty welcome. To this came the reply from Kensington:– "Very sorry, unable to take part in ceremony or travel. Please express my great regrets".

Shortly after one o'clock a large and fashionable company assembled outside the Lodge House of the new homes, the sun shining brilliantly, and making the function most pleasant. The children, who had been transported from Withington the previous day, were drawn in lines, and the band of the homes played selections. Mr C L Tomlinson, chairman of the Guardians, apologised for the absence of Lord Lorne but felt sure that everyone present, would be unanimous in their support for the famous Dr Rhodes whose duty it would now be to declare the Cottage Homes open. The architect, Mr J B Broadbent, handed Dr Rhodes an elaborately designed key to unlock the door of the probationers quarters. In turning the key, Dr Rhodes declared he was about to open the door, and hoped it would be the portal through which many a child would pass and come out again, fitted to enter upon a life of industry and usefulness in the future. On declaring the buildings open, Dr Rhodes and the other guardians led the great assembly of visitors including many residents of the Styal village, on a tour of the colony.

Dr Rhodes presided at the luncheon which served in the new school building at the village. The supporting guests at the banquet were:- Sir J W Maclure MP and Miss Maclure, Lord Mayor of Manchester and Mrs Gibson, the Dean of Manchester, Mr E H Greg JP, Mr and Mrs Tomlinson, Mr and Mrs Halliday, Mr and Mrs Jennison, Mr Ramsden, Mr Jenner-Fust (local government board inspector), Messrs Sargent, Pennington and Rostron, Mr and Mrs Bloomfield, Dr Orchard (Withington Workhouse), Mr and Miss Mainwaring, The Rev and Mrs Bates (Wilmslow), Mr and Mrs Sale, Dr and Mrs O'Doherty, Ald McDougall, Miss Greg, Capt Greg, Mr Broadbent (architect), Mr Howell (workhouse master), Dr Crowe (Cottage Homes medical officer), Miss Rhodes, Miss Appleton, Mr Brackly (master of Swinton Schools), Mr Normanton (contractor), Mr Blackwell (Schoolmaster at the cottage homes), Mr William Shaw (Superintendent). There were many representatives from boards of Guardians in Lancashire and Cheshire including Poor Law and School Board Inspectors.

Sir J W Maclure, Bart MP, called upon the company to drink a toast to the success of the Cottage Homes. The venture must be looked upon as a very great and a very serious trial; they could not tell what the effect would be until the homes had been in operation for a reasonable period. At Styal, the cost came out of the public rates, and therefore one wished the undertaking the greatest success. The carrying out of the scheme had been a bold stroke of policy, and one which they sincerely trusted would well stand the test of public criticism. The idea of removing children from places where they might become contaminated, to a better atmosphere, was many years ago attempted by the Manchester Guardians. They attempted to make the Swinton Schools as perfect as they could, but he was bound to say that the aggregation of a large number of children in one building was found to be a fault. The site of the homes had been well chosen although he felt that the Stretford division the most charming plot in Her Majesty's dominions. He did not think there was anything equal to Styal for health. He did not find any fault in the cost of the buildings, he thought them to be sumptuous. The only thing required to make them a success was not to let the children who occupy them get above their position. They must be taught to remember that they would face the world when they had served their time like any other ratepayer. They must not be indulged too much, and he sincerely trusted that the master would have full power to use personal correction when it was necessary, as it was when he was at Manchester Grammer School.

Dr Rhodes, on rising to respond, was received with rapturous applause. He believed that in establishing the schools, they were carrying out a statesman like, and economical policy. People made a mistake in classing all paupers under one head, there was the able bodied pauper, who was decreasing in quantity, year by year, and rapidly becoming a thing of the past, and who deserved no sympathy. Then, among the others there were the children. Many of such children were friendless, but he hoped that they would be friendless no longer at the Styal Homes. They had some of the gentry of Cheshire with them that day, and he hoped they would take an interest in the schools and in particular, the children. He maintained that from an economic standpoint, the Chorlton Guardians were perfectly right in the course they were following. Fifty years ago, England was the most pauperised country, but today very few countries could show the same independence and striving after thrift.

Dr O'Doherty, in his speech, proposed the House of Parliament, and said Sir John Wm Maclure should make representations to Her Majesty's government that another Sir John was required, namely Sir John Milson Rhodes. Dr Rhodes had done more than any man in the country for the bettering and salvation of the poor.

Mr Chandler proposed the "Lord Mayor, Corporation and City of Manchester". the Lord Mayor referred with pride to the satisfactory conditions of the city finances. While in 1888 there was a surplus of two and a half million sterling, there was now a balance on the right side of nearly four million. That he thought, showed them the representatives of the ratepayers had done the work entrusted to them very well.

After several more toasts to the "Visitors", "Architects and Contractors", "Ladies and other guests", the proceedings came to an end".

Chapter 7

THE SUNSHINE CHILDREN

Mrs Pankhurst's 'sunshine children' travelled only a mere five or six miles to their new home in the country, yet, they were the pioneers of the experimental cottage system and the ambassadors of the South Manchester Workhouse. Theirs was the task of setting the standard for the many thousands of children who would follow in their footsteps. they would be reminded from time to time that they were the luckiest children in Manchester, having been chosen to serve out their childhood at Styal and that they would forever be in debt to the Chorlton Guardians.

Sir John W Maclure, the Stretford Member of Parliament, had laid down the guidelines to the future administration of the Styal Homes during his speech at the opening ceremony as did his brother, the Dean of Manchester. The success of that day when Edward Hyde Greg made his appearance at the children's colony was recorded in the Wilmslow Parish magazine. "At length the children are in possession" went the article, "One of the charming days which have been so abundant this year enticed the good and curious people of Wilmslow to take advantage of the opportunity and they flocked thitherwood in large numbers". It would seem that everyone had reason to be well pleased at the events of October 4th. Maybe it was the balmy air of the Styal countryside or maybe it was the euphoria of the occasion, but whatever the reason, a great injustice had taken place on an indian summer's day. Not one reference or mention of Emmeline Pankhurst was made in connection with the Styal Cottage Homes and yet, apart from Dr Rhodes she had been the leading activist and the most ardent campaigner for the cause of the workhouse children.

Within weeks of their transfer, the children of Styal's new colony were well settled into a daily routine of schooling and domestic duties in the homes. It soon became apparent that the combination of experienced women from the workhouse and the well disciplined and institutionalised children would create the right atmosphere for a smooth and efficient run colony. Some of the home mothers such as Miss McMillan, Miss Boden, Miss Edghill, Miss Hoyle, Miss Cooley,

Miss Roberts and Mrs Widdowson had come to Styal by way of either Withington Workhouse or the Swinton Industrial Schools.
The surrogate parents to the colony's 320 children had settled very nicely and comfortably into their new houses, whilst Mr and Mrs Shaw had acquired a very important position in the employ of the Guardians but more to their liking would be the status afforded them by the workforce and the home mothers. The first term of the Superintendent had been marred by the sudden death of his youngest daughter, Belle, of diptheria at the age of six years. In keeping with the customs of the day, the Wilmslow Parish Church were requested to provide the necessary religious instruction for the children and also provide three church services every Sunday at the school hall near the Styal village. Styal Homes' first church services co-incided with the arrival of the new minister at Wilmslow Parish Church. His name was Mr H H Pitts.

In no time at all, Winter and Christmas - away from the workhouse - gave the new children of Styal their first taste of the festive season in the country. After the inevitable church service, the children were assembled in the school hall to receive their Christmas gift which had been provided by the Guardians. Each home had been decorated by the home mother and later in the day the children sat down to a Christmas dinner of roast beef followed by cherry pie and custard. A paper bag of sweets for every child concluded the Christmas celebrations and the Styal Homes Band, led by Mr Courbard, marched round the colony rendering their own interpretation of Christmas carols. A cold winter set in at Styal and the curtain was drawn across the gates of the children's colony. For the next month or two, the veil of winter would only be drawn to admit the guardians into the colony and to provide access for the older children who marched backwards and forwards to school.

The new colonials having survived their first winter in the country were now set to reap the benefits of a Styal springtime. The stillness of sleepy Styal was broken by the sun's warm rays and this was the signal for nature to explode and reveal to the former workhouse children the reason behind their presence. What Dr Rhodes and Mrs Pankhurst had witnessed in passing, now became the fruit for the children to savour. Like a new born taking its first breath, or like an animal awakening from winter's hibernation, the children rubbed their eyes in the warm sunshine and witnessed for the first time in their lives the wonders of nature. For the older children who remembered the workhouse background of yesterday, the sunshine homes at Styal became utopia. The quiet pastureland became transformed into a noisy landscape of birds, animals and insects, whilst the gentle breezes filled the air with earthly aromas of newly ploughed fields and smells from the two local farms. Even the colour of the landscape seemed to change before their very eyes. The statuesque trees of winter dressed themselves up in layers of greenery whilst the hedgerows sprouted new buds in every direction until their spring outfit was complete. Perhaps seen as the grand finale to the Easter parade were the clusters of spring flowers which grew along the highways and the byways and in the cottage gardens of Styal. The border to nature's shop window of Styal was perhaps the new grass shoots border which provided a sea of emerald carpet amidst blossoming trees.

During the year 1899, no fewer than fifteen deputations of boards of Guardians from all over the country came to the Styal Homes in order to witness the workings of the most modern children's village. One such visit, as recorded in the Wilmslow Advertiser, travelled from Stockport over the Easter period. 'The Mile End Guardians' desire to save the Poor Law children from the taint of the workhouse, a deputation of members visited Manchester, amongst other places, and visited the Chorlton Cottage Homes at Styal. Although acknowledging that the Styal Homes are perhaps the finest of their kind in the country, the deputations report is not favourable. Apart from the excessive cost, it was found that the children at Styal are isolated from the rest of the world. The Guardians are advised therefore, to adopt in preference, the scattered homes system as it exists in Bath.

Perhaps the two most significant visitors during the years were The Marquis of Lorne and Mrs Emmeline Pankhurst. Of the former, the Marquis was travelling to a Unionist meeting at Knutsford during the period of July. He broke his journey at Alderley for the sole purpose of paying a special visit to the Cottage Homes at Styal, where Dr Rhodes was waiting to give him a guided tour of the colony. the Marquis said that he was pleased with the Homes and would report his views to Mr Balfour in London. Mrs Pankhurst, no longer a Guardian, had sought the permission of her friend Dr Rhodes, before making the journey to the Homes. Although her visit went unrecorded, it must be assumed that her day at the colony was a day of mixed emotions. On the one hand, her reunion with the children she had known at the workhouse, now settled in a country environment, was rewarding in itself but the greatest reward of personal satisfaction was reflected in the healthy looking faces of her former charges. Inevitably her day at Styal echoed her own personal grief, for it was here at the colony that her pet cause had triumphed and circumstances had prevented her from witnessing what should have been her finest hour.

1899 produced many setbacks for Mrs Pankhurst including the crisis she went through financially. In this respect she was forced to abandon her house at Victoria Park, Rusholme and settle for a less expensive house near to the Guardian Headquarters at All Saints in Manchester. Not by choice, but from necessity she came to reside at No 62 Nelson Street, Chorlton on Medlock. In a sense, this move to within a few hundred yards of the Guardian offices, held some compensation. By chance, the position of Registrar for Births, Deaths and Marriages for the Chorlton on Medlock district had become vacant. It was at this juncture that Mr Jennision and his wife, knowing of Emmeline Pankhurst's plight, came to her rescue and offered her the position. If nothing else, the lowly paid post helped her over a crucial time in her life and served to rekindle the flames of political ambitions.

Mr Ralph Blackwell, a former headmaster of Rainow National Schools and formerly a teacher at St Augustines C of E school in Manchester, became the headmaster of the senior school of the Styal Cottage Homes. Compared with the usual standard of workhouse teachers, Mr Blackwell was outstanding. His qualifications for the post included no fewer than seven certificates which were Military Drill, Religion, Advanced Mathematics, Horticulture,, Woodwork, English, Advanced Sciences. The Chorlton Guardians had been extravagant in selecting Mr Blackwell and also very wise in using a man of his calibre to set the foundations of the educational system for the Styal children's seat of learning. Mr Blackwell was to remain at the school for another thirty years before his retirement. During this time, he and his family made their home at Handforth during which time he established himself as a parishioner , a local councillor and eventually, a justice of the peace. Right from the word go, the children of the colony nicknamed him 'Corky'. His wooden or cork artificial leg and his walking stick were his trademark to the thousands of pupils who came to know him over the years. Apart from Mr Blackwell, Mr

Shaw and Mr Courbard, the remainder of the staff at the colony, excluding the workforce, consisited of women. Whether it was a change in policy or plain simple economics, the House Father and Mother never materialised at Styal. Instead a small army of spinsters took over the day to day running of the homes and their word was law.

Sir J W Mclure's appeal for the local gentry to become involved in the Guardians colony, seemed to have fallen on deaf ears. However, for the first two years at least Mrs Greg of Quarry Bank and Mrs Greg of Oak Brow, both contributed some of their time and gifts at the school hall on the occasion of Christmas and Harvest Festival. Mr Edward Hyde Greg, having just recovered from the new pauper neighbours infiltration of Styal, was now incensed at the new rumour of the Chorlton Guardians intentions to bring yet another one hundred children to the colony. It became apparent that Mr Greg and the Guardians would never see eye to eye on any issue, but for Mr Greg, another greater and personal issue was threatening. A certain Mr W Sprowson of the village and an employee of Gregs Mill, Quarry Bank, was ordered to appear before the Macclesfield Magistrates Court to answer a charge of leaving the employ of Quarry Bank Mill without permission. Mr Sprowson was fined one pound and the case dismissed. After the hearing Mr Greg J P said it was a matter of principle. The sequel to this was that Mr Bill Sprowson had applied for a job at the Guardians colony and his successful application was seen by Mr Greg as a threat to his own workforce at the mill. The new competition for local employment at Styal was a new experience for the Gregs of Quarry Bank and was viewed with extreme cautiousness and the Superintendent and Mrs Shaw soon realised that they had more to contend with at Styal than just being the head of a large family. They found to their dismay that they were in the middle of the Guardians on the one hand and residing on Mr Greg's doorstep on the other. Because of the unbearable situation, Mr and Mrs Shaw adopted the role of peacemakers, their strategy being that if Mohammed would not come to the mountain, then the mountain would go to Mohammed. The opportunity to implement their future intentions presented itself almost overnight. Unfortunately, it was the death of Mr Greg's youngest brother, Arthur Greg J P of Bolton and Styal which caused a thaw in personal relationships, and the presence of Mr and Mrs Shaw at the funeral, was the beginning of a determined effort to make a peace with the Greg family.

The innocent children of the cottage homes were completely oblivious to the events at the village colony. Their daily and weekly routine of domestic chores and schooling and the strict observance of the Lord's day, kept them confined to their isolated existence behind the tall iron gates of the colony. It had been the intentions of the Guardians for the children to become more involved with the affairs of the Styal village, but somehow, the half mile which separated the two colonies may just as well have been two hundred miles. Whilst the homemothers co-habited with the village community, the fraternistation between the children of the village and the children of the South Manchester Guardians was non existent. In the complete history of the Styal Homes an impregnable wall of separatism reigned for the whole of it's existence. For the 100 orphans, the 150 children of broken families and the 30 children of unknown origins, the Styal family prepared themselves with a united display of optimism for what then had been described as 'a once in a lifetime' experience. The countdown to the 20th century was now in progress at both ends of the village but at the childrens colony, the accent was for the boys of the band to practise until perfect and every other child from the age of five years to drill to regimental order in readiness for the biggest event in world history.

The turn of the century was celebrated at the Homes with a dinner for every child which consisted of roast pork followed by plum pudding. After the feast, the children, in the wake of the Styal Homes Band, marched in a full military procession down the Styal road and in to the school hall where the band boys presented their well rehearsed concert. At the Oak school room, just 300 yards away, the two Mrs Greg's were organising their own concert for the village population. In spite of the efforts of Mr and Mrs Shaw to unite the two colonies for the new year celebrations, the recent planning application by the guardians to build more house for more children from Manchester had caused Mr Greg to reject the overture from the children's colony. For the boys of the Styal Homes Band, the realisation that they had reached a degree of proficiency soon became apparent. In a concert to commemorate the change over from the Chorlton Guardians to the new title of 'South Manchester Guardians' the band of the homes gave their first offical engagement. The concert, which took place at Withington was a dual purpose affair since the main theme was to raise money for the war effort in South Africa. Never the less Mr Courbard had good reason to be proud of his contingent of former workhouse boys who had shown the ratepayers of South Manchester, the proof of the Styal investment. For months to come, the main topic of conversation would inevitably revolve around the so called Cape war or Boer war and the Styal Homes band were to be called upon by various money raising concerts. As a curtain raiser to the onset of the first of the new seasons, the Superintendent and Mrs Shaw commenced with what was to become a ritual of annual social engagements their invitation to the Greg families and two hundred villagers of Styal to attend 'A Grand Ball' at the Styal Homes School was not only seen as a set showpiece, but also regarded as a command performance by the young musicians of the Styal Homes.

As each horse drawn carriage arrived through the school gates, the boys who had been selected as ushers showed the guests to the classrooms cum changing rooms. The Home Mothers, after weeks of preparation and dressed in their finery, lined the school hall in anticipation of an evening of dancing and feasting. For this important occasion, a handful of older girls from the colony had been picked to act as serving maids and attendents. Mr Mace the landlord of the Ship Inn at Styal, had been elected to serve the evening's banquet for which a charge was made. During the course of the after dinner speeches, Mr Shaw paid tribute to Styal's own hero who was serving his country in the Cape War. The Toast, was to Mr Greg's son, Captain R A Greg. Before the finale of the evening, a collection was made on behalf of the 'war relief fund' and the sum of £15-11-6p was raised.

With an increasing confidence, Mr and Mrs Shaw were presenting the child colony of Styal to the test of public opinion. The well mannered, well behaved and well regimented children were gradually alaying the fears which had preceeded their arrival in the neighbourhood. As proof of their acceptance, the Wilmslow Parish Magazine presented a feature on the Styal Homes, in its monthly edition. Even the Wilmslow Advertiser newspaper in a fair minded attitude of opinion had accepted that Styal Homes and the children were now a part of the Styal news column. Whatever picture Mr Greg had painted of workhouse pauper children, his theories and observation had been disproved. The childrem had come to Styal and yet because of their strict upbringing and their isloation from the world outside the gates of the colony, their presence was hardly noticable. Mr Greg, Mrs Greg, Miss Greg were all names which would become familiar to the children of the colony, mainly because Greg's Mill and the Greg family appeared to be the only topic of conversation of the people of the village. The House mothers and the staff of the Guardians colony, just by reading the local paper, would realise that any news under the Styal heading, was Greg news. Indeed, any stranger to the district could be forgiven for thinking that the Greg's of Quarry Bank and Styal employed their own press attache. Hardly a week would pass without mention of at least one of the Greg family. In the year 1900 for instance, one could learn that over a period of a few short weeks that : 'Miss Greg, whilst on a tour of India had been taken ill'; Captain Greg on board the City of Rome ship was expected in Gibraltar on his way to the Cape'; Miss Greg gave a lecture at the Styal Oak Schools all about her recent visit to China'; 'Capt R A Greg of the Third Lancs Militia is now at the Cape and reported to be in command of a Convalescent Depot at Norvals Pont'.

The so called scourge of Styal struck the village during the high summer of 1900 and to the residents of Styal it meant that Scarlet Fever had returned yet again. In an apology to the Church of England parishioners of Styal, the Rev Pitts of Wilmslow requested the Hollin Chapel worshippers not to attend the Cottage Homes church services. His carefully worded message in the Parish Journal stated :'It will readily be seen that the authorities at the Cottage Homes are anxious to use all means of prevention lest the epidemic should spread to the children there. Until further notice villagers cannot be admitted to the Homes colony'. The fever passed over the village and on this occasion the children of the cottage homes had been spared.

Harvestime to country people, holds a special significance since their livelihood is dependent to a certain degree, on nature's seasons and whims. The September harvest at the homes colony was not only a spiritual experience but also an affair with nature. For most of the year the children had observed the week by week routine of Norcliffe Farm opposite the colony and the adjacent Oakwood Farm which belonged to the Guardians. They had witnessed at close hand the workings of nature and the harmony of the elements. Trees had blossomed and borne fruit before their very eyes, whole fields had yielded crops of vegetables from tiny seeds, and such was the abundance of vast acres of corn, wheat and barley crops the whole landscape became a sea of tall grass land which swayed in the summer breezes. The sight of pastureland cattle and farmyard animals, became commonplace to the children but not suprisingly the farmyard and its multitude of livestock became the focus of attention. With an awareness of the true meaning of Harvest, the children and the home mothers of Styal spent two days preparing the school hall cum church hall in readiness for the big event. Just as in the previous year, villagers and friends came forward with gifts and flowers and vegetables whilst Mr Gleave of Norcliffe Farm and Mr Gradwell of Oakwood Farm became the main contributers of all kinds of farm produce. Mrs Greg of Oakbrow and Mrs Greg of Quarry Bank each sent a basket of fruit from their orchards. The young and recently married Mr Pitts concluded the third and final thanksgiving service of the day by paying tribute to the villagers and staff of the childrens colony. With pomp and ceremony out of the way, the small army of eager children spent the next hour dismantling and seperating the spoils of the harvest in readiness for their share of the booty in reward for their labour.

Styal Cottage Homes celebrated it's third Christmas at the school hall at which, visiting South Manchester Guardians were treated to a special concert by the well orchestrated musicians of the Homes Band. Before the children returned to the homes for a Christmas dinner and party, the Guardian delegation took turns in personally handing to each child, a small gift bearing the boy or girl's name. the Rev Pitts, in replying to criticism of the childrens Christmas at Styal replied: " The extra irrascible ratepayer calls this extravagance, we call it common sense and justice" . In concluding his comments he quoted the remarks made by the Local Board Inspectors, who had observed that 'the children are in excellent health and the absence of serious illness and of infectious diseases is unique, and speaks well for the staff and climate'.

A celebration of the first year in a New Century was held at the Oak Schools and Mr and Mrs Shaw were invited by Mrs Greg of Lode Hill to attend the function during the second week in January. The big gathering of the Greg families and the villagers under one roof provided the right atmosphere for an informal conversazione and during the course of the speeches a special reference was made to the two oldest working families of Quarry Bank Mill. Mr Venables and

Mr Hopley, both of whom had worked the whole of their lives from childhood at the Styal Mill, were each given a standing ovation. No sooner has the new twentieth century festivities petered out when the nation was dramatically plunged into mourning. The death of Queen Victoria on the 22nd January 1901, brought the country to it's knees and Styal, like every other village and township, went into grievous sorrow. Styal Homes Bandboys were again in demand as leaders of the procession of mourning. They lead the children and staff to the school hall for the memorial service and then proceeded round the perimeter of the village. For the whole of the march the big bass drum was shrouded in black drapes and an uneasy silence settled on the village as the children walked slowly back to their colony. No sooner had the echos of Queen Victoria's memorial service receded when a notice proclaiming the death of Sir John William Maclure arrived at the colony, resulting in yet again another period of enforced mourning. On this occasion, the band, with it's muffled drum preceded the entire staff and children of the colony and also a deputation of the children of the South Manchester Guardians, in a procession which was confined to the children's colony. In a speech to the occupants of Styal Homes, the Guardians reminded the children that Sir John, member of parliament for Stretford had been a very influential ally and friend of the former workhouse children and together with his brother, the Dean of Manchester, had helped bring about a better future for many people.

With the permission of the Guardians, Mr and Mrs Shaw announced their intentions to hold a Grand Ball, in the school room in aid of the war effort. The pre Easter official invitation resulted in yet another night of splendour, and there was no doubt that the Superintendent of the Styal Homes had initiated what was to become the main annual social event of Styal village. No fewer that 300 villagers and staff of the Homes attended the gala evening and big Mr Mace of the Ship Inn, provided the refreshments, permission having been given by Mr H P Greg. Two of the villagers who were employed at the Homes volunteered their services as 'Master of Ceremonies' and Mr H Walton and Mr T Middleton found themselves confronted with an evening which lasted from 8pm until 3am. Because of the late hours, the boys band had on this occasion been replaced by Mr Brooks and his orchestra from Wilmslow.

Styal village in 1901, was fast becoming a tourist attraction, thanks to the invention of the bicycle and the transport system which brought day trippers from Manchester to the suburban districts and even as far as the Cheshire borders. Newspaper correspondents in search of new territories for their nature lovers were now promoting Styal as the ideal day trip excursion for Easter and Whitsuntide. 'The road leads past cosy thatched cottages' went one report – 'meadows just now dappled with daisies and buttercups, orchards rich in pink and white blossoms, little woods from out of which bluebells flash upon the eye. Cottage gardens, all gems of green, white and yellow and one cottage displaying a hedge shaped like a peacock with it's tail outspread. The old Ship Inn, with it's swinging sign of a ship in full sail, the water fountain and the horse trough providing a watering hole for the weary traveller. Glimpses of small churches and village greens, thatched cottages and nursery gardens, were the borders to a walk with nature, ending at the cross roads where the old stone cross of Styal served as a resting place'. Another correspondent wrote:– 'The other day I paid a visit to the picturesque village of Styal. It was an ideal spring day. The genial rays of the sun seemed reflected everywhere, while a soft and soothing western wind made one feel it was good to be alive. From every hedge and tree the birds were pouring a flood of glorious melody whilst far above, almost out of sight, the larks sang as if their hearts would burst with joy that spring had come. The thatched and picturesque gabled cottages amidst the gardens and trees made one reflect on the wisdom and foresight of those kindly folk who laid out this beautiful garden village and found work for the villagers in their ivy clad mill at Quarry Bank. Surely it was in such a garden as Styal that the poet Herrick must have wandered when he wrote his beautiful poem "To Daffodils".

The swallows of Styal were as much a part of the village as every other insect, bird and animal. Their annual migration had brought them to Styal for hundreds of years but this particular year, a large proportion of the summer visitors ventured into the new children's colony where they adopted the eaves of each cottage for their new home. Needless to say, another link with nature was forged between the children and country wildlife. Whilst the year of the swallows would forever be rembered by the Styal Homes colony, the early birds of Summer turned out to be a particularly bad omen during 1901. Death a scourge which had plagued the workhouse year in and year out was still a memory to the older children of the Styal colony. They could recall the regularity of burial parties which frequented the buildings at Withington and more so, when in the midst of an epidemic. The Styal family, who had enjoyed three years of country sunshine were brought face to face with reality and a personal devastation. The dreaded Scarlet Fever which was common to Styal had once again invaded the village and penetrated the gates of the children's colony. Sometime over the Easter period amidst the background of lingering Easter hymns, and whilst the first swallows were building their new homes, the tragic news that two young children of the Styal family had died in hospital, filtered from house to house until everyone had digested the sadness of the moment. Meanwhile, the gates of the colony were closed to any outside visitors and the children became prisoners of their own isolation.

At the colony of Styal village, the epidemic had been more severe than the previous year and the timing could not have been worse. The scarlet fever outbreak had coincided with the deluge of day trip sightseers who rambled through the village and took advantage of the home made tea and cakes which were freely advertised on garden gates and cottage doorways. It was during this period of tourism, when pennies and threepenny pieces were exchanging hands in return for the delights of home made produce that Mr Edward Hyde Greg decided to make his stand.

On a Wednesday, the 22nd to be precise, in May 1901, a written notice was pushed through the letter box of every house or dwelling which was owned by the Greg families. It read :- "Owing to the continuence of scarlet fever in the village, I hereby give notice that I strictly forbid teas, refreshments or other accommodation to be provided in any of my cottages. Any tennant disregarding this rule will at once receive notice to quit". Signed E H Greg D L of Quarry Bank'.

When Mr Greg was confronted sometime in June about his recent ban in the village, he disclaimed any desire to tyrannise over the tenants. He said scarlet fever had been induced by drunken and undesirable visitors to Styal. He went on to say, that there was ample tea rooms in the village at the Ship Inn, owned by his nephew Mr H P Greg and the business was conducted on the strictest principles. What Mr Greg failed to disclose to the reporter was the previous history of Styal's scarlet fever plagues, especially the one which occured during the year his father Robert Hyde Greg died. Then, in 1875, Robert

Brierly the Lodge Keeper to Edward Hyde Greg of Styal Mill, was summoned by the Knutsford Santitation Authorities. He was found guilty of allowing his daughter Sarah Ann to attend school whilst carrying the disease and also allowing the mill hands to call in his house, knowing of his daughter's plight. The sanitation at Styal had come under a great deal of criticism during 1875 and according to one local newspaper; "the sanitation and smells at Styal were enough to knock a horse down". Again in 1882, a feature news headline read; " Styall is subjected to the Scarlet Fever again. The Inspector of the Rural Sanitory Authority states that the water supply to the houses is defective and infective and he attributes the evil to this cause".

Life had turned sour on the villagers in 1901. Not only had Mr Greg put an end to any cottage tenants making a few extra pennies to add to their meagre income, but as the dry summer wore on, so too did the drought and the inevitable fall in the water level of the river Bollin. With hardly enough water to turn the Mill Wheel, the mill hands were once again out of work or on short time. Just when the village of Styal seemed to be at a low ebb and when spirits were flagging, a message from Quarry Bank that Captain R A Greg was about to arrive home from the war, had the desired effect of turning a village of gloom into a village of celebration.

Captain A Greg the hero of Styal, came home to a tumultuous reception which began with his first step on to the platform at Handforth Station. It was reported that half of Styal village were awaiting his arrival and the scenes were chaotic, to say the least. Edward Hyde Greg had sent his own personal carriage to convey his son back to Quarry Bank but in the excitement of the moment, the horse was relieved of it's burden and the young men of the mill pulled the carriage all the way back to Styal with Capt Greg perched on his seat and waving to the cheering crowds along the route. A reception party headed by the Morley Brass Band gave a concert at the village and as a concession, the Ship Inn was allowed to serve more than the allotted two glasses of ale per person. During Captain Greg's absence, a poem had been written and dedicated to him by a youth of Quarry Bank Mill, although at a later date it was rumoured to have been conceived by a certain lady. For the benefit of the ensemble and those who had missed it's publication, 'The Styal Captain' poem was given a public hearing:

"Hurrah Hurrah for Styal, When they sent their Captain South,
Hurrah Hurrah for Captain Greg, Could be heard from every mouth.

Although the moon was rather dull, the crowd it gathered round,
To see it's bold brave Captain who, for southern climes was bound.

When up from Quarry Bank he came, his step was brave and true,
For he meant to fight for the British flag, the red, the white and the blue.

He quickly in the carriage got, as they moved along.
The band played 'Soldiers of the Queen' a most appropriate song.

And there he sat with perfect ease, as they drew him slowly on,
And every eye was straining, his face to look upon.

Their journey came unto an end, he in the carriage stands,
The crowd they gathered round him, to press his manly hand.

A specimen of manhood, his voice was bold and loud,
A smile played on his features, as he addressed the crowd.

And now with shouts and clappings, and noise of weeping loud,
He enters through the carriage door, borne by the friendly crowd.

And now we all must leave him, and hope and have a will,
That when he joins his comrades, they'll avenge Majuba Hill.

Farewell".

By contrast to the village, the children's colony had spent a comparatively quiet and subdued year but preparations were now taking place to enrol a workforce to help in building the new homes which were scheduled to be ready for opening within two years.

Chapter 8

THE WILDERNESS CHILDREN

Springtime, in the year 1908. a year which marked the first decade of the Styal family of children, would go down in history as 'the year of betrayal'. In ten years, the cottage homes had settled in to a set pattern, whilst the children had become accustomed to a well disciplined and authoritarian routine way of life. The last days and hours of those boys and girls who could trace their beginnings to the Withington Workhouse were now imminent. For them, the departure from Styal would mark the final chapter to a generation who had borne the brunt of the so called Styal workhouse paupers. At the very mention of pauperism, even though most of the children could not comprehend the meaning of the word, their heads would bow in shame and guilt. At the same time, many children quite rightly felt that they had taken the full advantages of the system of education and industrial training to warrant their new identity and dissociation from workhouse roots. Those caring Overseers and Guardians of the Poor Law in the Chorlton Union had, it seemed, carried out to the letter, their promises to house and educate the pauper children and to train them in a career which would benefit them on their return to the society of civilisation. No one could dispute that the former pale and delicate children of Withington were now strong in limb and portraying the rich complexion of a Styal country dweller. One question which must have crossed the minds of the more inquisitive children was why, at every springtime of this and every other year, did groups of children disappear from the colony just about the time that the first swallows winged their way over the Cheshire plains. To the female of the species who had learned from an early age the domestic, laundry and housewifery training, there were no delusions about their future role in life. All that concerned the girls, was whether they would become upstairs or downstairs domestics. Trained servant girls - especially the better qualified ones who came from Styal - were forever in constant demand and the Guardians found themselves unable to cope with the need for servant girls to the middle class applicants of Manchester and Cheshire.

For very obvious reasons, a much wider choice of job training facilities was made available to the boys of Styal colony. As future breadwinners in a man's world, it was a requirement that every boy should serve an apprenticeship in the varied choice of trades in the workshops of the colony. As in the girl's homes, boys too went through the rigours of domestic training but with the added incentive of a choice of trade within the cobblestone workyard area. It was within the confines of the work yard that such trades as baking, butchering, shoemaking, cartering, painting, gardening, farming, stoker and last but not least, musician, gave the boys a distinct advantage over the girls and a better all round preparation for the future beyond the front gates. Boys and girls alike, these first immigrants to Styal who had been pawns in an experiment, had not only repaid the Chorlton Guardians and the rate-payers with the high standard of success, but in doing so had set a high standard of obedience and discipline which could match any muster of soldiers on parade.

The regularity of children entering the gates of Styal and those making their departure had become commonplace over the years. However, now was the time for the strange phenomenon of Styal and it's eclipse with the centre of springtime. Within a matter of days, boys and girls from the cottages were informed that their departure was imminent and the destination was Manchester. On a quiet day of the week when all the colony children were behind their school desks and on a day when 'God's creatures were the only intruders on the Cheshire landscape, a group of 30 or 40 children aged from nine years to fifteen years assembled outside the house of the Superintendent. Mr and Mrs Shaw emerged on the scene and the children, having been brought to attention by the drill master, waited in anticipation for a farewell speech. It was during this short interlude that the name Canada was mentioned, along with the word 'emigration'. During the short ceremony and with a touch of excitement in the air at the thought of returning to Manchester, the two important words had little meaning. For the very last time, boys and girls, clutching a brown paper parcel of clothing and under the watchful eye of the drill master set off in the direction of Styal village.

The outside world often referred to by the children, was fast approaching with every footstep along Styal road. The girls, wearing traditional lace up boots and the long skirts and coats which had been made in the sewing room of the colony completed their appearance with a tie on bonnet. This moment of pleasure which came with the wearing of a new outfit was shared by the boys also.

They too sported new boots and stockings together with a knee breech suit of clothes and a cap. In the peaceful early hours of the day, the marching boots on the narrow pavement echoed a loud farewell to the Styal countryside. Blossoming fruit trees on Norcliffe Farm, and Cross Farm, waved their scented branches in the wake of the departing 'sunshine' children of Emmeline Pankhurst's yesteryear. Hoping for a glimpse of a friend, a pal, or even a sister or brother, the children marched on passed the school only to find that the morning lessons coincided with their departure. A right turn at the village to Stanneylands, signalled the last half mile to Handforth Station. Only the last remaining landmarks of Rose Cottage, Henshall's Smithy and Pownall farm, reminded the children of their Styal upbringing. Sadly to say none of the departing children had ever set foot in the actual village of Styal. Mr Greg had made it clear that he was opposed to the pauper children at the orphan colony, but more obvious to the older and knowledgeable people of Styal was the personal rift which existed between the South Manchester Guardians and the Gregs of Quarry Bank Mill.

Handforth railway station was now in view as the boys and girls neared the end of the military style march. The long and silent procession had provided the intimate and private interlude for each child to ponder upon his or her present and future. For many different reasons, it was a day when each child came to terms with a personal trauma and emotion, for tinged with the excitement of the moment, a deep rooted guilt complex common to each Styal Homes child united all in a bond of silence. Although the words 'pauper' and 'workhouse' were receding with the passing of time, some of the departing children had first hand knowledge of the Withington workhouse whilst one or two could even remember Mrs Pankhurst referring to them as; her 'sunshine children'. A day of warm sunbeams accompanied the children en route to the station and had helped to diminish the lingering doubts and fears. It was after all a day of hope and promise even if the future was uncertain. This was the day that Dr Rhodes had dreamed of. This was the day which Mrs Pankhurst had strived for. Above all else, this was the day when the final connection with the workhouse children was severed and the pauper image finally laid to rest. In what can be assumed to be the last farewell each and every child uttered it's own bon voyage to a country landscape which had been home during most of their young life. Many of the Children promised themselves that one day they would return to Styal, such was their gratitude for having started out in life in the Cheshire sunshine homes.

Manchester the birthplace of the majority of the Guardian children contrasted so vividly with the Chesire landscape that even the short marching distance between London Road Station and Strangeways left an impression which would be firmly etched in the minds of every child for years to come. The loud noises of a thriving day in the metropolis where people bustled their way between the ever moving traffic of horse drawn vehicles and trams, the shouting of news vendors and street traders, the echoes of clogs and horses hoofs on the cobblestone roads. The smells of Smithfield market on Swan street and it's awe inspiring complex of commercial food wholesaling, Styal and it's lingering scented atmosphere of springtime was now just a memory in the confused minds of the children, who, by the time they had walked to the district of Strangeways, could only wonder at the heavy ceiling of a smoke laden sky and a sunshine which had become pale and lifeless in its attempt to penetrate the murky Manchester skyline.

At long last, the procession was halted outside a large building, in Frances Street, Strangeways. Above the doorway were the words; 'Central Refuge Home' for the Boys and Girls Refuges. It was at this point that the last link with Styal was severed with the final farewell from the Drill Master, Mr Baker. From this time, fate was to play a major part in the lives of the Styal children, whose destiny lay 3000 miles across the Atlantic ocean. Mr Leonard K Shaw, the children's friend, was the founder of the charity run rescue homes. Since rescuing his homeless children from the slums of Deansgate in the late 1860's his christian mission work, together with the aid of voluntary and philanthropic subscriptions had mushroomed into a thriving Christian aid society. By the turn of the century, the Boys and Girls Refuge had established five boys homes and the much acclaimed Rosen Hallas home for girls. Each home was run by a surrogate mother and father and all homes were situated in the Broughton area of Salford. Another side of the work undertaken by the Central Refuge Home at Strangeways was the 'prison gate mission'. Here the voluntary workers would distribute food and clothing to the hundreds of boys and girls and men and women who were emptied back on to the streets of Manchester week by week. If the Refuge Mission could obtain just a few hundred signatures, in pledges to christianity and the total abstinence of alcholic beverage, then this alone was sufficient to warrant the claim to success. The final appendage to the operations of the Refuge Home and also the reason for the Styal boys and girls now on its doorstep was it's claim to be the Manchester agency for exporting and emigrating children to the domain of Canada.

For some unknown reason, the child emigration programme of 1908 was behind schedule. Normally as had been the case for the past twenty years, the boys would have departed the shores of England during the middle of March, so as to be ready to be put to work on the Canadian farmlands and also coinciding with the last snows of Canada's long winter. Likewise in a repetitive sequel of routine, the girls would follow in the footsteps of the boys exactly one month later and take up duties as farm servants or domestics.

Mr Stephens lost no time in explaining to the Styal children that they had been chosen by the Guardians as being very special, in that they were being given a much better life in Canada, a land full of promise and opportunity and unlimited sunshine. They were the ambassadors of the Manchester Guardians and as such, Manchester would expect them to repay their debt to society by working hard on the farms and attending a place of worship on every Sunday. Without any goodbye, the girls were separated from the boys and taken to the Rosen Hallas Home to begin a month's training as servant domestics. The boys, having been given a small cardboard box or suitcase bearing their names and number, each recieved a change of warm clothing and a prayer book. Before the day was over, the Styal boys of the Manchester Guardians found themselves integrated with other boys of all ages who had similar backgrounds and from different districts of Manchester. There was no mistaking the excitement at the prospect of the travels which lay ahead. Before retiring for the night, the complement of seventy boys were informed by Mr Stephens that the following day would be the most important day of their lives and also the last time they would see Manchester.

The shy, reserved and institutionalised children of Styal would forever remember their departure day from Manchester. Breakfast, a packed lunch and inspection parade, and finally the trek across Manchester to Central Station. In crocodile formation, the boys observed Manchester Cathedral and Chethams School as they walked in the direction of Deansgate. People stopped to stare as the marching boys walked up John Dalton Street to Albert Square. It was at this point that Mr

Stephens informed the boys that the Lord Mayor of Manchester wanted to say goodbye to them. After filing into the Great Hall of the Town Hall, the boys were stood to attention whilst his worship gave a speech and then handed each boy a new silver shilling. In the wake of all the farewells, the boys continued their short journey across Peter Street and on to the platform of Central Station. The huge stationclock indicated to Mr Stephens that the Liverpool bound train was still some time away and he allowed the boys to take their last look around the perimeter of the station . Sometime in the early afternoon the group of boys, still clutching their boxes and parcels disembarked at Lime Street Station. In this strange city which resembled Manchester, the only address which the children had been given in case they became seperated was: Mrs Birt's Home at Myrtle Street, Liverpool. Like the Boy's and Girl's Refuge in Manchester Mrs Birt's was a refuge home that was also deeply involved with the emigration of boys and girls to Canada. The Home was used as a staging post for children from different parts of the country en route for Canada. During the course of the evening after a meal and various inspections, the boys were once again on the move to what turned out to be the quayside at Alexander Docks. The ship which was taking them to Canada was not setting sail until the next day but in any case, the excitement of the day had taken it's toll and the weary travellers soon fell asleep on the mattresses which had been conveniently placed in a wharehouse near to the quay.

During the early hours of a wet spring day, the Styal children, together with the many other boys who were sailing that day, faced the final reality of saying goodbye to their homeland. As the high tide carried them further out to sea the deep rooted feelings and emotions surfaced long enough for teardrops to well up and mingle with the salty spray of the sea and wind. In those few moments when the gaze was intent on the receeding Liverpool shoreline, there were those who questioned themselves as to the real reason for their departure. Some, who still carried the stigma of workhouses and pauper parents, put their fate down to that reason. At least, nobody in Canada would be able to point a finger at them. There, their secret would be safe. Yet others, quite logically in the cold light of a new day, could present many arguments without answer. If for instance, the Guardians were their parents why were they being sent to Canada ? Why couldn't they have stayed and worked in Manchester ? After all, they had a mother somewhere and there were brothers and sisters and aunts and uncles who would have taken care of them. The older boys from Styal Cottage Homes had reason to feel bitter, in more ways than one. Most of them had trained as joiners, painters, cobblers, plumbers and gardeners. They had been promised apprenticeships in Manchester where they would become self supporting, many with relatives to whom they could have turned. With every shipload of human cargo, the same questions must have been asked time and time again. Next month, the parties of servant girls would be facing the same dilemma and asking the same questions. Just a handful of Styal boys and girls could remember being referred to as Mrs Pankhurst's 'sunshine children'. Surely, she could have helped them, she took them out of the workhouse. Perhaps it was just as well that children were naive of politics and politicians for the departure of the Styal children had coincided with imprisonment of Emmeline Pankhurst in Holloway goal.

The young children and teenagers who were emigrated from Styal to Canada can only be viewed as another episode in the history of Styal's long standing connections with the poor and orphan children of Workhouses. Styal Cottage Homes and their superintendent were quiet blameless of what appeared to be a well orchestrated plan of deportation. So too, were the village onlookers who, in their ignorance of government legislation, could only wonder at the wisdom of banishing and exiling children from their country of birth. Chorlton Union and the South Manchester Guardians, along with boards of Guardians throughout the country, must share in the responsibilites of committing their young charges to a life of slave labour in the Dominions. In the main, most boards of guardians shared the same reluctance as Dr Rhodes, in releasing their adopted children for the foreign labour market. However, government policy being what it was and the Local Government Board Inspectators always on hand to carry out to the letter, the ruling on emigration, there was little chance of the children escaping the system.

In the year 1784, the same year in which Samuel Greg opened his first cotton spinning mill at Styal, an institution began in Australia which was to span a period of 84 years. On board a ship which left England in 1868, bound for the Australian continent, a small group of convicted men and women were to make history as being the last of approximately 16,000 convicted men, women and children who had been exiled to the penal colony. As one door closes, another opens; so goes the saying. Exactly one year after the cessation of Australia's cheap labour supply, a new era opened it's doors to a hitherto untapped market in the export trade. Quite by accident rather than intention, an English woman who had been running an agency for the supply of trained female labour to the vast farmlands and townlands of Canada and America was confronted with a request to supply young girls of tender age who could be put to work as domestic servants or farm maids. The first cargo of English children set sail for Canada sometime during the year 1869. Maria Rye, the woman concerned, had been very careful to choose only the best girls from various workhouses through the country. One such workhouse which provided the first fifty girls for Canada, was the Liverpool Workhouse Schools, at Kirkdale, Liverpool. They were joined by other girls from London to start their historic voyage which would take them over 3000 miles to a place in Canada called Niagara.

From that time on, over a period of fifty years, the busy sea ports of Liverpool and London were to export no fewer than 80,000 boys and girls of all ages. Some children were as young as five but in the main the ages ranged from eight years to 14 years. The destination for the majority was on the small homestead farms of southern Ontario which was roughly half way across Canada, between British Columbia on the Pacific side and Newfoundland on the Atlantic side. Quebec, New Brunswick and Nova Scotia also profited from the child immigrants, as did the cities of Montreal and Toronto. Following Miss Rye's commercial venture into the thriving market of child domestics another lady by the name of Annie Macpherson, personally escorted her first shipload of boys to Canada where the majority of the youngsters were deployed on farms in Ontario. The Macpherson girls of Glasgow in Scotland, were to become famous as missionaries to the hundreds of homeless children of London's East End and the city of Liverpool. Annie Macpherson, the youngest of three sisters, had established a Rescue Home in the East End of London for the waifs and strays and the Dickensian street urchins. It was during the many trips to the docks at Liverpool that prompted the leading citizens of Liverpool to ask Annie Macpherson to set up a similar rescue home in their city. Early in the summer of 1873, a home was opened for the waifs and strays of Liverpool by Louisa Birt, Annie Macpherson's older sister. The third Macpherson sister, Rachel stayed with Annie and helped in the administration of the child rescue homes. In the many years during the late 19th century and early 20th century, many philanthropic societies and institutions were drawn into the child emigration market, including the Boy's and Girl's

Refuges of Manchester and Salford. Perhaps the most famous and successful institution on record is that of Doctor Barnardo. Drawing on the experience of Annie Macpherson he began his first Mission Home in the East End of London. By 1872, having sent many of his rescued children to Canada through the well established Annie Macpherson route, he himself embarked on his own system of emigration and in a short time, the flamboyant Dr Barnado was systematically shipping out his own boys and girls to his homes in Canada. In his short and burdened lifetime, Dr Barnado transported approximately 45,000 children to the farmlands in Canada.

The receiving home in Canada for the Styal children, was a large detached house called 'Marchmont'. It stood in it's own ground with a driveway, just within walking distance of the city centre of Belleville, Ontario. Marchmont had been given to Annie Macpherson by the town council of Belleville in 1870. A keen and dedicated follower of Annie Macpherson was an English woman by the name of Ellen Agnes Bilbrough. In later years, she married a church minister and became Mrs Wallace. Ellen Bilbrough took charge of the Marchmont Home in 1870 and from that moment on, Manchester established it's connections with Belleville, Ontario. For the next forty five years, a steady stream of orphaned destitute, workhouse and pauper children would make the annual migration journey from Strangeways to Belleville. There was one exception to the Manchester and Belleville association, the cause of which was a clash of religious backgrounds amongst the children. In the main, the emigrants to Canada consisted of children from Protestant denominations and as such caused no problems to a system which was dominated by the all powerful Church of England administration. It would appear that no provision had been made to emigrate children who belonged to the Roman Catholic church but one such organisation came to the rescue, in the cause of the Manchester workhouse children at Withington. Very little information exists in regard to the deportation of Catholic children and the only reference to this minority group is the emigration reports of the Chorlton Workhouse at Withington. This register of children's names started in the year 1888 when a large consignment of children left Withington to be handed over to the Manchester and Salford 'Catholic Protection and Rescue Society'. From this base at Bishop's House, Salford, their future destination was somewhere in Quebec, via Liverpool. It is a sad but true fact that many of the early immigrants who were put to work on the vast farmlands of Ontario were rarely visited or supervised and as such became orphans again, in a big country where they were forced to cope with their own destiny. The Catholic children of Manchester were to face this ordeal and many others. Perhaps the most disturbing ordeal for the young boys and girls was their arrival in the French speaking province of Quebec. Records from the Chorlton Union, list the names and addresses of the French Canadian farmers where the children were deployed but the column which should record the all important progress report of the children, is completely blank. This short sequence of events surrounding the catholic children of the Manchester workhouse, has no ending. What became of those young lives under their new masters will never be known.

Historically speaking , the events of the child labour emigrants to the provinces of Canada, have conveniently remained out of reach of general knowledge publications. If one seeks this information one has to resort to searching out the archives of city libraries or delve into ancient newspapers. The story of the Styal children and the South Manchester Guardians represents only a fraction of a monumental biography of child emigration. The beginnings date back to King William the Fourth when an act was passed during his fifth year of office. Entitled: 'An act for the amendment and better administration of the Poor in England and Wales', it was continuously quoted by the Local Government Board Inspectors. The all important wording lay in a sentence which read: "Be it therefore enacted that it shall be lawful for the Guardians of any Union or Parish to expend money in and about emigration of any poor or deserted child under the age of sixteen years who may be chargeable to their Union or Parish".
Another person who campaigned strongly in favour of child emigration, was the Liverpool Lord Mayor, Samuel Smith Esq. It was Samuel Smith, in his office as Mayor, who opened the Louisa Birt Emigration Home in Myrtle Street, Liverpool. However, as a member of parliament, his platform lay in the House of Commons where his eloquent speeches in favour of child emigration were to receive the support he wanted. In 1887, Samuel Smith moved a resolution respecting the emigration of pauper children to Canada. His impassioned plea to the house, painted a picture of vast farmlands in the provinces where thrifty peasantry abounded and where thousands of farm homes without children pleaded for child immigrants.

As is always the case in politics there was another side to the emigration coin. A statistical paper published in 1895, which closely resembled a company balance sheet, showed a total of 82,000 children who were situated in Reformatories, Industrial Schools, Union Workhouses and Paupers Schools. The annual cost of keeping these children was one and a half million pounds. In this same report, it reccommends the Industrial schools children as being:'better off in the Colonies and a great saving to the public would be effected'. Another paragraph goes on: "Of all the 52,002 children in workhouse schools, 14,354 were with their parents in the Union. There is little doubt that many of these would be better off seperated from their parents, but there are grave difficulties in the accomplishment of this. There would be no difficulty whatever regarding the remaining 37,648 who are all orphans or deserted children. The majority of these could be gradually transfered to Canada. They are not criminal children, merely poor children.

If the average stay of each child in the Union five years before it can become anything like self supporting, the total cost to the country for these children reaches no less a sum than £3,764,800. Let us presume that only 30,000 of these could be emigrated, the cost would be thus:-

30,000 children at one years maintenance Workhouses at home at £20 per head	£600,000
Emigration expenses of children at £15 per head	£450,000
	£1,050,000

But the public funds would be immediately relieved of the permanent maintenance of thirty thousand children. There is an official love by our Boards of Guardians for the building of many large establishments for their children. There is a parochial reluctance to imbibe new ideas, a want of faith in the virtues of emigration, and a good humoured aversion to the banishment of thousands of boys and girls from their own land. In conclusion, we would like to impress upon the burdened ratepayers of England that to encourage well regulated and well oversighted juvenile emigration will undoubtedly prove economical from every point of view."

Many are the stories which have been told of the child immigrants of Canada. Some, tell of the luck and the appreciation of having been given the chance of a better life in a better country. Others will share bitter memories of a cruel life and poor conditions on farms which paid little or no money for long hours of slave labour. Every emigrated child who had thrown away the shackles of the workhouse and pauperism, was to be subjected to another type of humiliating experience in the Provinces. Because of the adverse publicity the British children had received over the years, an expression had evolved which, when uttered, caused a feeling of guilt and shame. The new Canadian immigrants adopted their new title as: 'home boys' or 'home girls' and with it the inexplicable stigma which was to accompany them well into adulthood.

As promised, most of the boys returned to Styal, albeit a lot sooner than they had ever imagined. They came for a last lingering view of faces and places and of a home where they had tasted a feeling of security in their short lifetime.

The years of the 1914-1918 war brought a steady trickle of uniformed soldiers who, like their Canadian countrymen, were en route for front line duties as members of the Canadian Expeditionary Forces. It is ironic that the Great War was responsible for giving the 'home boys' of Canada, the chance of a brief encounter with former relatives and friends with whom they had lost all contact. Sad too, is the fact that many hundreds of those young soldiers would never return from the battlefields of Europe. During a confused childhood ending in emigration and a teenage life of drudgery as Canadian immigrants, the soldier boys had never risen up to the first rung of the social ladder. Now, the status of the volunteer soldiers had changed dramatically. Yesterday's 'home boy' was today's brave soldier and as such demanded honour and respect, the distiction and importance, the rank and glory, all of which contributed to the most rewarding of all, that of self dignity.

On reflection, Styal Cottage Homes and its child emigrants to Canada programme was brought to the attention of the public at large, time and time again during the year of 1908. Again, the circumstances surrounding the disclosure of events and dialogue carried the usual overtones of political motivation. The ominous date of Friday 13th

March became a day of significance, for on that day a spark of rebellion was spelled out in the headlines of a leading Manchester newspaper; "Should the Chorlton Board of Guardians send children to Canada ?" - 'The question of child emigration cropped up again at the meeting of the Guardians on Friday. Mr Park protested against the terms used by some of the Guardians. In his opinion, it was far better for the children to be shipped out to Canada than to be allowed to drift back into family associations. Mrs Garrett declared that to send children out to Canada, was sheer exploitation. the conditions in Canada she believed, were such that were they known in their entirety, every Guardian would blush for shame that they ever sent a child abroad. Mr Skivington said the children were simply sweated by the Canadian farmers and at eight or nine years of age were sent on to the farmlands. The life was simply shocking . Mr O'Loughlin pointed out that there was no child in the present batch under 12 years of age. Miss Olga Hertz said that the heated arguments were an electioneering ploy. She said that children in Canada wrote home saying how happy they were.'

The Wilmlsow Advertiser of April 10th recorded the following:-

'At the Chorlton Board of Guardians meeting. Mr Skivington and Mrs Garrett both made strong protests on the subject of Child Emigration to Canada. After previous complaints Mr J Obed Smith, Asst. Supt of Emigration said in reply that although some cases had failed, the children were better off in Canada. Mr Skivington said he had letters and details of children from seven and eight years upwards who were hired and working on the basis of employee and employer. Mrs Garrett said they were fighting a great principle. It was not right to send children out to another country to live and be employed under conditions which were illegal in England. They should not economise at the expense of a child's life.

Another newspaper report on May 1st headed it's feature 'Styal Homes Children For Canada' 'A heated discussion over the proposal; to send more children to Canada, took place at the Guardians first meeting for new members. Dr Garrett and Mrs Garrett and Mr Skivington opposed the proposal on the grounds that the children were too young, and that children in Canada were employed when too young. Dr Garrett said that the sending of young children to Canada was an evasion of the law by the Guardians. Miss Hertz explained that the Manchester Refuges at Strangeways sent children to a receiving home in Canada and then the children were placed on farms. Reports of the children were sent back to the Guardians. the motion was carried.'

'Chorlton Guardians - Children and Canada' This bold heading of a major article which concerned the Styal Children's colony appeared in the Alderley and Wilmlsow Advertiser towards the end of May , 1908. It records in great details the last known interchange of words between the Guardians and the Canadian Emigration Department. Mr Obed Smith acting on behalf of the Canadian Government, accused Mr Skivington and Mrs Garrett of not being in any position to back up the statements they had made on Child Emigration. In addition, he wished to call their attention to a special report which had been compiled by Mr G Bogue Smart, chief inspector of British emigrated children to Canada during 1907. Although six deaths had been recorded of children aged between six and thirteen, the majority of children enjoyed good health. Mr Skivington in reply, said 'what they took exception to, was the emigration and employment of children of tender years - seven, eight, nine and ten years of age' Mr Smith wished to point out that they had made other statements. Mrs Garrett remarked that there was not a single word she had said that could not be justified. She maintained that children, some only in their second standard , were sent out to Canada to earn their own living. That, in her opinion, was as bad as in the old days, when children were brought in the cartloads to the Lancashire factories.'

There is no doubt whatsoever that an obituary on the slave labour children of Britain who worked on the Canadian farms would produce a most distasteful chapter in the annals of the Poor Law system. An abundance of material evidence exists on both sides of the Atlantic to verify the claims of some of the Guardians of the poor. The charge of 'child slavery' had been admitted by high ranking officials as far back as the 1880's but unbelievably and only two decades into the 20th century, a government minister of Canada admitted that cheap labour was still entering the country under the guise of philanthropy. In 1924, an agreement was finally reached between Canada and the United Kingdom, that children of school leaving age only be emigrated.

Many are the charges and accusations which can be levelled at those responsible for the misery of those emigrants, but in the final analysis, the blame falls fairly and squarely on the British Government. Double standards and double dealings were self evident with every cargo of child labour destined for the Dominion of Canada. The fixed price of £10 per child, under a government subsidy often reached £15 or £20 by the time the children reached the shores of Canada and many prominent business people made a lucrative living from a continuous flow of emigrants. Even in the Canadian provinces, bonuses were paid to agents and agencies at an agreed rate of a few dollars per head. As long ago as 1840, children who toiled in British factories were given the right to receive a part time education. In 1893, the Education Act made full time education compulsory for all children up to the age of fourteen. This hard fought for progress on behalf of the poor law children was an issue which became very conveniently overlooked in the case of the thousands of emigrated children to Canada. For six months of the year the 'home boys' and girls were deprived of any eduaction due to the all important priority of the Canadian farming economy, but even within the allotted six months which were set aside for schooling, only a small proportion received any education due either to the severe winter conditions or the restrictions of the employers who could readily find enough work on the farms to warrant absenteeism.

Styal Cottage Homes, Supt. Residence.

Styal Cottage Homes, Main Avenue.

Chapter 9

'A SCOTTISH SOLDIER'

Some dates and some names will forever be carved on the historical landscape of Styal village. Even to this day there are a few stalwart octeganarians who remember a day in the year 1911 when, insignificant as it seemed, the large iron gates of the Styal Homes colony were opened to admit the brougham carrying the guest of Mr and Mrs Shaw. The only clue to the identity of the man who stepped down from the carriage was his appearance and manner. The straight back figure, the marching steps to the doorway of the superintendent's house, and the military salute, were enough to proclaim the arrival of the new Bandmaster cum Drill Instructor. His name was John Cochran. No man in the history of Styal could match the outstanding achievement of John Cochran and for the next twenty eight years, he was to build for himself a reputation which would make him a legendary figure, both at the South Manchester Cottage Homes and in the Greg's village of Styal. Mr Cochran's arrival at the settlement had come in the wake of a euphoria which had held the children in a state of excitement for most of the summer months. Although the occasion had gone, the Coronation Sports programme celebrating the newly crowned King George V, had been celebrated at the two colonies of the village in their own separate presentation. The bunting and the regalia had long since returned to storage but the memories of extra rations of bread and jam and cakes and lemonade, would remain uppermost in the minds of the children. Long hot summer days were not so unusual on the Cheshire landscape and Mr Cochran must have been delighted with his future prospects at Styal under the clear blue skies and the gentle wafting breezes of the approaching harvest time. According to the local newspaper, Styal, like many other Cheshire landscapes, was undergoing a period of official drought and unlike the previous year, the river Bollin had been reduced to a trickle.

The Styal Cottage Homes of 1911 had altered little in it's thirteen year history. True, there were now 400 children in the colony as opposed to the original 300. Discipline was more severe than the workhouse era and the children's work schedules at the Homes had increased with the years. For those who had escaped the deportation to Canada, a unique group of older children experienced two coronations during their Styal upbringing. If they could remember the year of 1902, a major event took place at Styal village at which the Styal Homes Band were given their first ever official engagement. The occasion, as recorded, was The Coronation Sports of 16th August 1902. A huge turn out of the local villagers, including the Greg families, were entertained by the Styal Homes Band during the day and evening. Many prizes were won by many local people - went the report. Mr Greg's personal rift with the Guardians of the Poor, had it seemed, established a permanent wedge between the two colonies. Only through the peacemaking overtures of Mr Shaw were the band boys of the orphanage able to mingle with the Styal village folk. Almost to the day, one month earlier, Mr Balfour the M.P. for Ardwick in Manchester, was appointed Prime Minster cf England. On that day on the 12th July 1902, Mr Shaw took great delight in explaining to the community of the colony that the Rt. Hon gentleman had laid the first foundation stone of the Styal Cottage Homes and that the memento took pride of place at the boardroom of the Guardians at the Superintendent's house. Another foundation of a different kind was established that year at the Styal village. Mr Shaw further enhanced his associations with the Greg family by receiving a personal invitation to serve as the secretary of the newly formed 'Village Club' under the presidency of Mr H.P. Greg.

'The Steam Navy used in constructing the new Railway continues to travel in the direction of Styal. It makes headway slowly, it is true, but it will reach Styal sometime in the future'. This notice which appeared in the Wilmslow Advertiser during May of 1903 was an indication that progress was on the horizon for the isolated colonies of Styal who were dependent on the horse and carriage, or simply by walking to the main shopping districts of Handforth and Wilmslow. It became obvious to the Guardians that Styal would benefit from a major railway link to Manchester and Wilmslow and especially during 1902 and 1903 when traffic in and out of the gates of the colony increased substantially. Not only had the building programme for the new cottages at the colony gone well, the work force were well ahead of schedule due mainly to the weather conditions. Amongst the many local observers of the activities taking place at the Cottage Homes were two young men of the village. One, Alex Gradwell, was the youngest son of Mr Gradwell who tenanted the Oakwood Farm on the Chorlton Guardians Estate. The other young man and best friend of Alex Gradwell was Walter Hope. He too was the son of a local farmer who was a tenant of Mr Greg's estate. Mr Hope's family had farmed Cross Farm for many years, so much so, that everyone referred to the smallholding as Hope's farm. Apart from the personal loss of two young sons, Styal village bade farewell to the two young boyhood pals who had made the bold decision to emigrate to the farmlands of Canada. Just a few weeks prior to the official opening of the new cottages at the colony, Alex Gradwell and Walter Hope departed from Styal in search of fortunes on the Winnepeg farmsteads of Manitoba Province.

Doctor Rhodes and Dr Jayne the Bishop of Chester, had shared the same platform on many occasions both in the cause of the workhouse conditions and improvements in the Poor Law system. Today, Tuesday, October 27th 1903, they were the guests of honour at the opening ceremony of the new homes at the Styal Intitution. Before an audience of all the colony children, including the latest 130 inmates, Dr Jayne, supported by Dr Rhodes, addressed the South Manchester Guardians and prominent clergy of Wilmslow and Manchester. He regretted the fact that no members of the local gentry were present but hoped that in their absence he could rely on their support for the success of the enterprising venture at Styal. The Band of the Homes, under Mr Courbard's leadership, escorted the Bishop round the colony and on his return to the platform he duly signed the visitors book. Mr Pennington, the chairman of the Guardians, explained to the Bishop that the Colony system of looking after the children was comparatively new and had only been decided upon after much thought, research and experimentation. There were complaints, he admitted, on the excessive costs of the Styal experiment but he was sure that the public authorities after a few years would judge the Colony systems to be the most economic. The chairman asked the Bishop to observe closely the children who now stood to attention behind the little ones. Their physique was simply phenomenal. He knew that there was a great scare at the present time about the deterioration of the national physique. A Royal Commission had been sitting, but he wished that commission would come to Styal and observe the results of town people being brought up in the country. Dr Jayne, in replying to the chairman congratulated the Chorlton Guardians on their selection and speculation at Styal which had been thoroughly thought out and well devised. Cheshire could have no reasons to complain, because they had what was now called a garden city in their midst.

In the long history of workhouse and institutional reformatories throughout the country, one piece of unwritten legislation was claimed by the Poor Law Adminstrators as a constitutional right. The custom, was for every institution to create its own brass band. As in the case of the Styal Homes Band, whose beginnings dated back to 1885 and whose first young musicians were recruited from the Oakum Picking Shed of Withington Workhouse, three ex-army Bandsmen had nurtured it's progress until the final and continued destination of Styal. Mr Courbard, the third bandmaster/drill instructor, now the forerunner of the Styal Homes Band, was held in high regard by the Chorlton Guardians. In their opinion, his skills had contributed to the present status and reputation which brought about the mounting demand for the Band's services. Not only was this proving to be a valuable asset in advertising the success of the experimental colony to the Manchester ratepayers, they were seen as ambassadors to the village of Styal and Wilmslow and surrounding areas. Mr Grimshaw, a member of the Styal Homes Guardians sub committee, had foreseen the day when the band would benefit from a new identity image and to this effect he proposed to his fellow guardians that an application be made for membership of the Church Lad's Brigade. On the fourth day of July 1904, the band of the Styal Cottage Homes colony, was offically accepted into the 6th Battalion of the Manchester Regiment Church Lads' Brigade. From that day on, the band, already disciplined at a high standard, took on a military identification which not only entrenched their academic standing but implanted a corner stone at the colony from which a new breed of Christian Soldiers would emerge.

In many ways and for many reasons the community of Styal village would remember 1904 as a year of great opportunity. Throughout the vicinity there was talk of great prosperity and jobs becoming available either at the Styal Homes colony or in connection with the new railway link which was making steady progress towards Styal. The men of the village were aware of the fact that before any link up with Wilmslow or Manchester could be achieved, it would neccesitate the building of a huge viaduct accross the Dean valley at Handforth. Ironically, Quarry Bank Mill made some headway into the 20th century by receiving the first supply of gas to the village of Styal. The timing could not have been better for Mr Greg for, the river Bollin had almost dried up during the summer and short time working was yet again operational. About this time Mr H.P. Greg, in a last bid to find the culprit who had stolen his 100 pheasants from his Styal residence, boldly displayed a 'Reward' notice in the windows of his Tea Rooms at the Ship Inn but even the size of the reward failed to draw any response.

The smart blue uniform proudly worn by the new C.L.B. of the Styal Homes Band were on show to the public's gaze for the first time at the Norcliffe Sunday School's annual sports day festival during the August holiday period. Mr Shaw, the superintendent had been given the captaincy of the C.L.B., and on his first outing at the Oak Schools, his first commission included the duties of guard of honour to the visiting Bolton Board of Guardians including Mrs A Greg, a serving Poor Law member. In the wake of yet another successful Harvest Festival, Mr Shaw received the news that the Guardians were coming to the Styal colony on the following Friday to perform what they termed a 'ceremony of great importance'. On the day in question, the horse drawn carriage drove through the gates and pulled to a halt in front of the Board Room. As the dozen or so Guardians alighted from the vehicle, Captain Shaw's salute became the signal for the Homes Band to burst into an interlude of military music, whilst the C.L.B. and the remaining masses of children were brought to attention. As spokesman for the South Manchester Guardians, Mr Grimshaw stepped on to the dias clutching a seemingly enormous silver cup. He revealed quite proudly to the 450 children the handsome Cup now on display, had been purchased from donations subscribed by former boys of Styal Homes who now lived and worked in Canada. To show their appreciation for what had been done for them, they requested the Guardians to purchase and present a silver cup to the Colony at Styal and for the Cup to be awarded to the winners of a football competition, to be held annualy between all the Boys cottages. In handing the Cup to Captain Shaw, Mr Grimshaw requested that as a reminder to future generations, the silver trophy should be know as the 'Canada Cup'.

Christmas and New Year, also proved to be a time of mourning throughout Styal during 1904 and 1905. On Christmas Eve the First Lady of the Cottage Homes - Mrs Bloomfield - died and within the same week Mrs Edward Hyde Greg of Quarry Bank, passed away. In the usual manner, the children of the Homes colony marched along Styal Road with bowed heads, the silence only interruped by the beat of the muffled drum. Progress and proficiency was the theme at Styal Homes during the long hot summer of 1905. For the very first time, an annual sports day was instituted, when the boys and staff of the colony competed for prizes. Two weeks later, the month of June having run its course, the iron gates were opened to admit the whole battalion of the Manchester C.L.B. As new members of the Brigade, Styal Homes played host to the various battalions who had arrived from Tiviot Dale and were about to pitch their tents for a weekend in Cheshire. Amongst the guests were representatives of St. Pauls Church, Brinnington and Chorlton on Medlock. St. James of Gorton, and St. Clements of Chorlton cum Hardy. At the annual camp held under canvas at Prestatyn for one week, the Styal Homes boys excelled to such a high standard that they were chosen by Field Marshall Sir George White to represent the whole North West battalion by playing the music at the Officers' Mess dinner party.

'Friday March 16th - A group of boys are ready to leave the Styal Cottage Homes en route for Canada' Yet again, emigration was rearing its ugly head as the springtime of 1906 got under way. True to form, a party of girls was despatched one month later, their destination being some 4,000 miles from Liverpool. Both these dates made the columns of the local newspaper where they came second place to the usual mass advertising for Eastertime. Down at the village, in the wake of the echoing Easter hymns, the Ship Inn became the focal point for what was to become known as the 'Mace - Middleton' wedding. Crowds of guests began the day with a wedding breakfast at the Ship Inn Tea Rooms before moving on to the Wilmslow Parish Church. At the ceremony, Miss Mace of the Ship Inn became Mrs Middleton of Peacock Farm Styal. Another wedding of greater dimensions brought the looms of Quarry Bank Mill to a temporary halt and to the village, a public holiday. On a Tuesday when the days were growing shorter and with Harvestime just around the corner, Captain Alexander Greg J.P. fourth son of Edward Hyde Greg J.P., married Miss Alice Mildred Worthington, an employee of the Quarry Bank Mills and a resident of Dean Row, Wilmslow. The wedding took place at the Alderley Edge Parish Church. One week prior to his wedding, Capt. Greg attended the much publicised funeral of his uncle, Mr R.P. Greg, J.P. of Norcliffe Hall, Styal. It was disclosed that Mr R.P. Greg had left an estate worth £83,000 plus Reddish Mill and real estate. Styal's Scarlet Fever plague invaded the colony once again, but on a high note , the year ended with the expected good news of the railway viaduct at Handforth. 'At last, the new rail bridge is completed' went the report in the local paper - 'and Styal is one step nearer to its own link with Manchester and Wilmslow'.

Miss Megan, a local inhabitant and a lodger of Mr Allman, a worker at the Cottage Homes, died during the Spring of 1907. Apart from being the oldest person in the community - aged 94 years - her roots could be traced back to the early days of the 'Apprentice House' where she began her career at Quarry Bank Mill at the age of six years. Her 79 years at Styal had witnessed three generations of the Greg Masters. In an obituary, it was said that she had outlived all the apprentices except two. The following year, in another exposé of Styal's oldest inhabitants, it was revealed Mr Moore, Mr Allen, Mr Venebles, all octogenarians, had begun working at Greg;s Mill at 8 years of age and had worked from 5-50 a.m. until 6-30 p.m. In the winter, the hours of work were extended to take full advantage of the higher waters of the river Bollin. Mr John Hopley received the highest accolades and an Easy Chair for his "remarkable instance of long service" in the employ of Robert Greg & Co., of Quarry Bank.

Styal Homes Boys' Band were notching one success upon another, with every passing year. Their high standard of proficiency as musicians and Drill Cadets was earning for them a reputation second to none. The demands for the Band's services was reaching statistical records out of all proportion. For the second year in succession, the band of the Styal Homes provided the music for the annual Garden Party at Norcliffe Hall. Mr Greg and his family were the hosts to the Ladies and Gentlemen of the district who were invited to the Whitsuntide gathering where the famous Norcliffe Rhodedendrons provided a landscape in full bloom. A Manchester correspondent on a visit to the Cottage Homes wrote 'The 510 children, who now utilise ever scrap of accomodation, are drawn from the poorest class of the community, the offspring of those who have broken down under the stress of life's rugged journey; the product of the slums, and the destitute. The band is the greatest institution in the homes, its reputation has spread far and wide. It plays very well and it plays a very useful part. It provides the music for the Church Lads Brigade of the district and other functions. It is also a happy hunting ground for regimental bandmasters from all over the country who are constantly on the look out for good musicians Some of the old boys of Styal are now prominent musicians in His Majesty's Army and they know the best source for likely recruits. Mr Grimshaw readily admitted that the Styal Homes were an expensive item in the expenditure of the Guardians but also agreed that they were the finest of their kind in the world'. By coincidence, the local newspaper of the following week carried a headline: "The Expenses at the Styal Cottage Homes" In this article the Guardians were replying to their critics and especially to the accusation of being "the most extravagant Board in the United Kingdom." Mr Skivington commented on the criticism that the cost per child at the Homes was 14 shgs per week, and added that "this was not expensive compared with other institutions". Mr Bloomfield remarked that the cost of training and maintenance amounted to five Shillings and sixpence per week excluding the cost of land and buildings.

Mr Skivington, mouthpiece of the independent Labour Party and a newly elected member of the Chorlton Guardians, followed in the footsteps of Emmeline Pankhurst. Whenever there was a cause, Mr Skivington stood in the front line. In one particular instance at the first meeting of the Guardians after the summer recess, Mr Skivington made the strongest possible objection to the Board's decision to transfer 30 children from the Styal Homes to the Hornchurch Union in Essex. He said the children had been adopted by the Chorlton Guardians and it was unfair on the children to have them removed from their families in Manchester. The opposition spokesman for the Guardians said that they would still be under the careful eyes of the Guardians and that the parents of these children were unfit to have them or be near them. The removal was in the best interests of the children. Mr Skivington had unwittingly and in all innocence put his finger on a very sensitive area of child administration by the Guardians. For the past three decades, Unions of Guardians had quite freely transferred children to and from, all parts of the country. Such was the intricate and usually complicated systems of covering their child transfer methods, any inquiring parents or relatives would find it almost impossible to trace an offspring. Another twenty five years was to pass before this practice came to an end and within that time, Styal and Manchester became the disembarkation centre for the disowned boys and girls of Hornchurch and Ipswich Boards of Guardians. Likewise, the South Manchester Guardians despatched their adopted children to the Townships in Essex. In one final outburst before Winter's curtain was drawn across the village, Mr Skivington, in reply to Councillor Kay's remarks that "within the palatial surroundings of the Styal Homes, boys were being taught the violin and the piano". said "It was a compound, concentrated concoction of arrogant ignorance. The public who knew how the children were treated at Styal, would never swallow that".

In retrospect the year 1909 will be catalogued as one of the most important in Styal's history. After nine long years of planning and hard labour, the LN & WR railway, opened its link line to Manchester, via Wilmslow. If ever Styal needed a shot in the arm, this was that moment and that year. Ever since February, short time notices had been pinned up at the Quarry Bank Mill, informing the workforce of 'bad times' ahead. As yet, most of the workers especially the mill girls from Wilmslow were unaware that they would be laid off for most of the year, owing to the installation of the new Northrop looms. The country in general was still in a state of mourning after the Lancashire coalmining tragedy of the previous December when, 75 men and boys of the Maypole Pit of Wigan were killed. Mr Jones, in his first ever function as the new full time Chaplain of the Cottage Homes, performed a service of remembrance at the school hall which was attended by the Homes children and the village folk. A concert by the Bandboys helped to raise £28 towards the 'disaster fund'.

On a blustery weekend in late March when 14 children left the colony for the embarkation at Liverpool, the villagers of Styal were informed through the local press that the post of Station Master has been awarded to Mr James Henthorne of Bramhall L. & N.W. Station. He is expected to take up residence at the newly built Station Master's House during April, prior to the arrival of the first locomotive. The foundations to the Station Master's house were built over the remains of what had been the Horse Shoe Inn. In its heyday, the Horse Shoe Inn had hosted the annual Styal Flower Show, whilst its competitor, the Ship Inn, catered for the annual Celery and Vegetable show. After the death of Ellen Downes in 1876 the business was carried on by her son, James Downes until its closure in 1879. If any one year is prominent in the history of Styal , then 1879 deserves a special feature. The New Year began with the arrival of the first village policeman, namely P.C. Pettingall who wasted no time in proving his first case against two of the villagers whom he had caught redhanded. He apprehended Henry Hope and William Spencer drinking alcohol at the Ship Inn on Christmas Day. At the hearing, the magistrates cautioned Mr Hartley, the licensee of the Ship Inn and dismissed the case on payment of costs. During February, a 'Highway Robbery' took place down Twinney's Brow, the unlucky traveller being Mr Tongue. Meanwhile , at the village, a notice had veen pinned up at the Mill, informing the 400 to 500 workers that a ten per cent reduction in wages would go in to effect almost immediately. Progress manifested itself at Styal during July, when a branch Post Office was formed in the village. The Office, situated at Mr Taylor's of Farm Fold, came under the jurisdiction of the main Post Office at Handforth and Mr Taylor's son became the rural letter carrier. In the finale to 1879, Joseph Hartley, inn keeper of the Old Ship Inn, was forced into liquidation after a term of three years at the Ship. His brewing business together with the house, outbuildings, fixtures and fittings and the residue of the fourteen year lease, all went under the hammer at an auction at the Swan Hotel, Wilmslow. The Old Ship Inn, with a yearly rent of £90 was sold to Mr Wignall of Hilltop, Wilmslow for £879.00.

On Saturday, May 1st 1909, the first train to arrive at Styal, bound for Wilmslow, drew to a stop and was greeted with a musical display by the band of the Styal Cottage Homes. There was a last minute rush to buy tickets for the new service to Wilmslow and the first ticket issued by Mr Henthorne, was to Mr Mace's son of the Ship Inn. Amongst the few passengers who alighted from the train that special day, was a young man by the name of Frederick Victor Smith. At the age of twenty one, with a newly acquired Poor Law school teaching certificate, he had arrived at Styal to take up a teaching position at the Guardians' Poor Law School. May's importance was further emphasised by the death of big Mr Mace of the Ship Inn. Although his links with Styal were comparatively new, his nine years at the village had earned for him a reputation as 'caterer extraordinaire'. In fact, it was Mr Mace's catering abilities which first brought him to the attenting of Mr E.H. Greg whilst catering for the Cheshire Army Regiment at the annual Volunteer Camp. Mr Greg was so impressed with his talents and personality that he promptly invited Mr Mace to apply to his nephew, H.P. Greg, for a post at the Ship Inn at Styal. In later years, Mr Mace's daughter - Mrs Middleton would return to the place of her birth in her new capacity as Licensee of the Old Ship Inn.

"Death of Dr John Milson Rhodes". This was the headline to most Manchester newspapers on Monday the 1st October 1909. The Doctor, in his 62nd year and showing the tiredness of a person twenty years older, died suddenly at his home on Saturday evening, September 29th. The tributes to this great man poured in from all over the country. They came from all types of professions, mostly medical and Poor Law adminstrations, including the three Unions of the Manchester Boards of Guardians. His funeral from Emmanuel Church, Barlow Moor Road took place on the Wednesday when, as a sign of respect, all the businesses and dwelling houses drew their blinds in mourning. A mass of wreaths and posies lay in the doorway of his surgery which stood on the corner of Wilmslow Road and Whitechapel Street. The business of Kendal Milne of Deansgate, Manchester admitted at a later date that Dr Rhode's funeral at the Southern Cemetry Crematorium 'had been one of the biggest in their history as undertakers'. Many were the speeches that day and most of them by very eminent people. Perhaps the most simple and meaningful obituary, is the plain inscription which is engraved on the monumental clock and drinking fountain which still stands in Didsbury village, "A Friend to Humanity". At the Styal Colony, the usual proceedures for mourning had taken on a special meaning for the man who had not only founded the Cottage Homes, but who had been revered as the Father of the Children's Colony. The funeral procession of 460 children, claimed the whole width of Styal Road as they walked slowly in step to the tune of the Dead March. This day and occasion had quite rightly been claimed by the Guardians half of the village, who were in no doubt that the achievements of Doctor Rhodes should never be forgotton.

Within two months of the departure of Dr Rhodes, Styal's other father figure and master Edward Hyde Greg, met his death at the age of 83 years. The enigmatic squire, the former adversary and combatant of the Manchester Guardians, signalled the end of an era, with his passing. Accordingly, the age old custom of bowing heads and doffing caps by the Poor Law Children of the Homes to E.H. Greg was brought to an end. If for no other reason, the band of the Cottage Homes could be relied on to give a professional service where funerals were concerned. No sooner had they played out the late Edward Hyde Greg, when their services were in demand for another important engagement. This time, the meaning was more personal. Mr J.H. Baker, the Band Master of the Homes, died at the age of 43 years. During his short life he had spent 22 years as an Army Bandsman before becoming a Workhouse Instructor in London. For the past four years he had lived in Alma Lane, Wilmslow with his wife and six children and had been a leading member of the Wilmslow Philharmonic Orchestral Society. Exactly one week later, on May the sixth, 1910, the proclamation of King Edward's death was given. Not only were the children paraded behind the Band to the village Cross, but most of the villagers gathered to hear the fanfare of trumpeters who sounded the Last Post. Peace and tranquility seemed to be the keynote for the remaining half of the year except for one hiccup which brought the village out of its shell. During September, the River Bollin from Carrs Wood to Styal had flooded to such an extent that there were genuine fears of damage to the Quarry Bank Mill and the subsequent loss of work. The memories of the older generation could describe in great detail the so called Great Floods of 1872, when the raging waters of the Bollin had flooded the Mill, covered the looms and washed away the cotton.

In comparison with the previous Bandmasters and Drill iNstructors, ex Sergeant Trumpeter John Cochran, No. 3007 of The Royal Scots Grays, began his service at Styal Homes with a thoroughness which spelt perfectionism in his duties as a Bandmaster, and fear, for the children who were about to taste his brand of Army discipline. In today's society, Mr Cochran would have been cateogorised as: 'a legend in his own lifetime'. He was – according to his own testimony – brought up by an Aunt in Brighton, who was herself, a refugee from Ireland and a victim of the Potato Famine. At the young age of thirteen, and excitedly impressed by the recruiting campaign of a Cavalry regiment, he enlisted with the Royal Scots Grays and received the Queen's Shilling. By the time John Cochran had reached his 25th birthday, he had mastered every musical instrument of the Regimental Band and one year later became Sergeant Trumpeter, Had he wished, he could have gone on to become the regimental Band Leader but preferred instead, the ranks rather than the Officer's Mess. As a soldier, he was engaged in action during the Boer War of 1900 – 1903 where his active duty saw him in battle at the Transvaal Orange Free State, and the Relief of Kimberley. For this episode, he was awarded the Queen's South African Medal. His second medal, the King's South African Medal 1901 and 1902, was his reward for two long years of service at the front line. The customary Medal for Long Service and Good Conduct, was awarded during his last year of service in 1909. This was the year in which John Cochran obtained the position of Drill Master cum Band Master at the well known Duke of York Military School in dover. Although his Army career was almost finished and new horizons were beckoning Sgt. Trumpeter Cochran would come to regard his last two months of service with the Royal Scots Greys as the most important and rewarding, in his lifetime. At a special concert which took place on the Royal Yacht which was at anchor in the Solent, Mr Cochran, in full dress regalia and conducting the Regimental Orchestra, regarded the occasion as probably his last public and farewell performance. On that Midsummer's evening, after the last of several encores, the celebrated guest of honour walked across the Ballroom and stopped face to face with Sgt Cochran. Slowly and deliberately, the uniformed V.I.P. took a medal from his tunic and pinned it on the tunic of the surprised Band Leader. He then saluted him and thanked him for what he described as the best concert he had ever witnessed. One month later, before leaving his adopted country of Scotland, Mr Cochran received a letter from Buckingham Palace, informing him that His Majesty had given him permission to wear the Russian Gold Medal for Zeal which had been given him by the Emperor of Russia, for his mastery of music.

For obvious reasons, the year of 1912 will always be remembered as the year of the Titanic. At the Homes Oakwood Farm, Mr Gradwell, the tenant of many years, passed away. In his place, the Guardians appointed a young man by the name of Robert Park, and with it the official title of Farm Bailiff. That same year, a young nurse at the Homes Hospital received a promotion and became Sister Donovan. Six years later, the two newcomers to Styal, were married and became Mr and Mrs Park of Oakwood Farm. 'Death of an Old Resident'. There was nothing unusual about this caption which frequently occurred in the obituary columns of the local paper except that the year of 1912 signalled the end of the so called 'grand old man of Styal'. Mr George Venables of Oak Cottages had celebrated his 90th birthday with his lifelong friend Mr Moore, some months earlier. His death, now a few weeks past, had brought to light many facts about his ancestry which had supposedly begun at Styal in 1787, a time when his forbears had been one of the 280 chldren who had worked the 14 hour shifts. The descendants of the Venables family are still in evidence in the village of Styal, but perhaps unknown to the family or the general public, is the amazing coincidence of the name Venables in relation to Styal. As far back as the 17th century, when Styal's pastures and woodlands followed the upstream course of the River Bollin as far as Wilmslow, the whole landscape belonged to a family, known as the De-Venables. Owing to a tragic accident and the subsequent drowning of eight year old Richard Dc Venables the only son and heir, the estate was duly left to the two daughters. One of the sisters married into the De-Trafford family, whereupon the land became divided. In time, the remaing sister married and became a Booth of Dunham Massey.

Within the first three years of his leadership, Mr Cochran not only improved the Band's performance and discipline but also swept the board by winning five major trophies for the Styal Homes Band. At a rally for the North West Battns, of the C.L.B. The Colours were awarded to the Styal Band by Canon Rees. Yet again, the Styal Band took the first prize at a meeting at Manchester's Free Trade Hall when, in honour of their professionalism, General Sir Henry Mackinnon requested them to take the stage for the evening's performance. Even the village profited from Mr Cochran's talents. Not only was he asked to take over the new look Styal Village Orchestra, but also, to organise concerts at the Village Club. A regular weekly advertisement offered the Band's services for all types of occasions. Such was the pleasure and appreciation of the South Manchester Guardians with their Band Boy Ambassadors, a first time treat was given to all the children of the Colony, by way of a cinema show at the Public Hall at Wilmslow. In a mammoth procession on a Saturday during 1913, the Homes Band led the marching children to Wilmslow for their silent picture show. For the majority of the children, this day's outing was the first time they had been allowed out of the Colony, apart from their daily march to School and Church. If Mr Cochran had earned acclaim for his leadership and musical talent, the rewards were just. On the other hand, his brand of discipline could be viewed from two angles. To a Band Boy, or a member of the Church Lad's Brigade, he was a Sergeant Major of the worst pssible kind. To the everyday boys and girls of the Homes, Mr Cochran, dressed immaculately in his buttoned blue uniform and peaked cap represented a person who instilled fear in the mind of every child, especially when he carried his stick.

The Styal String Band played out the year with a Grand Concert at the Village Clubroom. Its members included: Band Leader John Cochran, Pianist Mr Bone, Violinists - Mr Sprowson and Mr Sumner. Other members included Mr Allman, Mr Gradwell and the latest newcomer to the orchestra:; Albert Scott, a protege of Mr Cochran and Cornet player with the Styal Homes Band. At a gala concert during January of 1914, the Homes Band gave their last performance under the leadership of Mr Cochran. Unknown to the children, Sgt Trumpeter Cochran had been requested to rejoin his former Regiment in Scotland. Amongst the guests that evening, was a certain gentleman from the Manchester and Salford Refuges at Strangeways. His name was Thomas Ackroyd and his purpose for attending the concert, was to raise money for the Emigration to Canada scheme. At the end of the evening, Mr W. Earlam of the village, handed him a collection which amounted to £7.17.8d. It is significant that either due to the onset of the Great War, or the end of an era, the year of 1914 became the last year of Child deportation from the Styal Cottage Homes. Out of a total of nine boys and girls to leave the Colony, two in particular can claim to be the last to leave Styal en route for Canada. Fred Smith aged 15 and Christina Jackson aged 16. set sail at 8 pm from Liverpool, abord the 'SS Alsatian', both of them, leaving behind brothers and sisters. In charge of that party of children destined for the Marchmont Home at Belleville, Ontario. was Mr Thomas Ackroyd, secretary of the Frances Street Refuges. His other charges from the Manchester Charity Homes of George Street,

Salford, included : A. Kelsall, John Smith, George Conboy, Reg. Pickstone, and D. Cocker.

1914, turned out to be a particularly progressive year at the Guardians Colony. In contrast, Alex and Earnest Greg of the Styal village, were witnessing the rapid decline of the once famous Quarry Bank Mill. For Major Alex Greg J.P., personal tragedy brought sympathy from the villagers when the news broke concerning the sudden death of his young wife Mildred, the former Mill employee and friend of many local people. Meanwhile, Styal Railway Station was host to a very special train which had arrived on the morning of Wednesday, July 8th 1914. The Military Band of the Homes, as they were now referred to, paraded on the platform to welcome the first ever visit of a Manchester Lord Mayor on official duty. Also on the train were the parents of children in the Styal Colony who were also making history by becoming the first parents to visit their children on what in the future, would become known as: 'the Annual Parents Day' visit. In the wake of the visiting officials who had departed for the waiting reception at the Homes, another contingent who had alighted from the train, marched down Styal Road under the guidance of their escorts. These, were the children and the charges of the Manchester Guardians who had come on a day's outing and especially, to meet their parents. Boys and girls of all ages had come from Holly Mount Schools, Bury, and Buckley Hall Orphanage, Rochdale, whilst the Tiny Tots had arrived from the Dr Rhodes Memorial Home, Didsbury.

Just as sure as the rumblings of war were spreading through Europe, conflict of another kind was already showing itself in the various Board Rooms of the Guardians of the Poor of Manchester. As the days progressed at the Sunshine Colony at Styal, it became apparent that the Lord Mayor, Alderman McCabe and the Mayoress, Mrs O'Neill of Manchester, were spearheading a strong deputation of high ranking officials from their own committees and institutions. The Manchester Guardians were well aware that the children of Styal Homes were probably taking part in the last official funtion under the auspices of the South Manchester Guardians, formerly the Chorlton Guardians. After many years of political wrangling, an order was finally received from the Ministry of Health, for the consolidation of Townships. In effect, the South Manchester Guardians and the Prestwich Guardians were to lose their identity and amalgamate with the Manchester Guardians under one Union and the date of the takeover had been set for the 31st March 1915. After a luncheon at the Boardroom, all the dignitaries were assembled for a speech by the Lord Mayor. In it, he was very careful to avoid the issue of the amalgamation of the Unions, saying "as he had never taken part in the discussions with regard to the annexion of the Manchester Unions, he had better remain silent". What he did remark on was the beautiful location of the Homes which in his opinion, was more like a high class Boarding School. He also made the comment that it should be the purpose of every right minded man or woman, to make the life of the child as happy as it could be, so that memories of childhood days should be happy and uplifting. He believed also that the children at Styal got advantages which unfortunately many working men could not give to their children. Early to bed and early to rise, together with good food and discipline made the children physically fit and better than their counterparts in the slums of the city. Before leaving the lawn on that hot summer's day. Ruby Lewis, a girl at the Homes, presented a bouquet to the Lady Mayoress. The rest of the day consisted of a sports competition between the children of Buckley Hall, Holly Mount, Dr Rhodes and the Styal Homes.

Chapter 10

'THE MANCHESTER GUARDIANS'

Styal, like most other towns and villages throughtout Gt. Britain, would never be the same after Autumn 1914 and the beginning of the Great War. Almost overnight the village hummed to life and became the junction of constant trafficing of uniformed personnel and civilians. The declaration of a recruiting compaign by Capt. Greg was not unexpected and its effect on the village was a slow awakening to the nationalistic war cries for a volunteer Army. Almost from the start, rumours had been circulating in the village regarding the erection of a top secret Concentration Camp and as such, anxiety and the impending war, turned Styal into a hotbed of speculation. Not until October did it become official that there was to be a Concentration Camp, but more to the relief of the locals, the location had moved away from the village and was to occupy the old Dye Works at Handforth. Even as early as the first day in October, a telegram had been received in the village, with news of it's first casualty of the Great War. Mr Bone, the Baker at the Co-op shop of Oak Cottages Styal, was informed by the 1st Cheshires, that his son William who lived at Seedley and was married with two children, had been reported missing whilst in action with the British Expeditionary Forces. Had it not been for the escape of a German P.O.W. during November, the activities of the new Internment Camp on the border of Styal would have gone unnoticed. However, this incident brought to the attention of the public, the reasons behind the top secutiry around the village and also the information which revealed that there were now over 1000 aliens in the Camp. Although Handforth's new residents were veiled in secrecy and security, rumours about the Camp were rife in and around Styal. The newspapers admitted that during December, Max Weber aged 42, had taken his life during his brief stay at the Camp. Before coming North, Mr Weber, a Hungarian and an itinerant musician, had lived at Torquay. By the end of the year, almost 1500 people were being detained.

Locally, it was announced that a Grand Patriotic Concert in aid of the poor in Belgium, was to be given in the Styal Cottage Homes Schoolroom on Friday 11th December. The Chairman The Rt. Hon. Lord Mayor of Manchester, would be in attendance accompanied by the Lady Mayoress. Amongst the many artistes, would be the guest appearance of Monsieur Firman Swinnen, organist of Antwerp Cathedral. The Children of the Homes were to give a dancing display whilst the Band would provide the music. At the end of the evening's concert, a spokesman for the Manchester Guardians announced that sixty former boys from the Styal Homes were prisoners of war and one was in a Manchester Hospital for wounded soldiers.

Not only was the Styal Homes School at the village in use seven days a week, being both a school and a church, it became by virtue of it's size, the focal point of the village whenever a large meeting place was needed. Perhaps one of the largest gatherings ever recorded at the School took place during April 1915. On a Friday evening and after weeks of publicity, a 'Public Meeting' for the purpose of recruiting, drew hundreds of local people of the area together with the boys of the Colony. On the stage, surrounded by the Homes Band and the C.L.B., Mr H.P. Greg J.P. and Col. Ernest Greg, both presented their plea for Styal as a whole, to go forth and fight for King and Country. Further inspiration was given by Major Richard Rigg of the Border Regiment who was the evening's guest speaker. One of the Homes boys who signed up that night was 17 year old Albert Scott. Besides being the leading Cornet player for the Band and a Sergeant in the C.L.B., he was a member of the Styal 'Village Club' Orchestra. Almost to the day, one month later, Pte. Albert Scott, a former orphan and latterly an employee of Bollin Hey Farm, was fatally wounded whilst in action with the Border Regiment. His death became the first of many, amongst the former Boys of the Styal Homes. The influence of Sgt. Trumpeter John Cochran was still very evident in the day to day running of the Homes, even though he was back in service with the Scots Greys. From his base at Edinburgh Castle, he conducted a recruitment campaign which was not only beneficial to his own regiment but other Scottish regiments. During his five years of the Great War, he was responsible for the transfer of over forty boys from the Homes Band, to be enlisted as Bandboys of Scottish Army Units. The following names are but a brief insight into Mr Cochran's choice of Styal Orphans who in his opinion, were all potential Bandsman and ambassadors of the famous Styal Military Band:

'1915 Bandmaster of the Blackwatch donated two guineas for the enlistment of Daniel Murray and Robert Hobson, both 15 years of age.

1916 William Partington age 14 and Alfred Piper age 15,

enlisted into Band of the Argyle and Sutherland Highlanders.

1916 William Bolland, William Walters, Samuel Dawson, enlisted in the 1st Sutherland Highlanders, all aged 15.

1916 James Webster age 15 years, joined the Royal Scots Greys Band.

1917 Arthur Doyle and Thomas Mather age 15, enlisted in Band of the Royal Scots Greys.'

'New Church for Styal Cottage Homes' - 'First Church of its kind in England'. These dramatic headlines, which appeared in the Wilmslow Advertiser during March, were the prelude to what had been described as a most unusual 'foundation stone laying' ceremony, by the South Manchester Guardians. On Wednesday March 5th 1915, Mr Joseph McGrane, chairman of the Homes Committee and in the company of Miss Olga Hertz, vice chairman, laid the Foundation Stone on a patch of open ground which lay just inside the Colony gates and directly opposite the Boardroom of the Guardians. After laying the stone, Mr McGrane informed the vast audience that the day and the occasion was unique. "Firstly, Styal would be the first Cottage Colony under the Poor Law Authority to have its own Church. Secondly, and even more unique - (his own words) is the fact that the individual who has been honoured by your request to perform this ceremony, is a member of the Roman Catholic Church." In declaring the stone to be well and truly laid, Mr McGrane was presented with a silver trowel by Mr Overmann, the architect of King Street, Manchester. The Rev. Mr James, in performing his first ever service as the new Chaplain of the Styal Homes, spoke of the new church as a future landmark and sentinel at the gates of the Colony.

Nine months later and at a cost of £4000 the Church had been completed by the workforce of Messrs Burgess and Galt of Ardwick Green, Manchester. The builders incurred a loss, due to the rising costs of materials caused by the War. The Guardians refusing to pay any more than the agreed contract. The Church, built to hold 620 people, held its first service on Tuesday, 30th November. On that day, not only were the 509 children of the Homes in attendance but also, members of visiting Boards of Guardians, including Doctor and Mrs Garrett. The dedication of the new chapel was directed by the Bishop of Chester. His Lordship commented on the workmanship of the new building and also on the architecture of the half brick and half timber, as in the old Cheshire style. During the ceremony, the Bishop informed the congregation that the Church would not be named after any saint and that the use of the Church would be confined to the Children of the Homes.

Handforth's Concentration Camp was rumoured to be bursting at the seams by the time Easter had settled at the village. The 235 survivors of the German ship "Blucher", which had been sunk in battle, had recently arrived from Edinburgh Castle and had swelled the numbers of the overcrowded Camp out of all proportions. However, the situation resolved itself one month later when it was reported that a total of 900 German civilians and Aliens were being deported from Styal and Handforth to Fleetwood, where they would sail for the Isle of Man. For the remainder of the War, it was not uncommon to see gangs of German P.O.W.'s working on the farms of Styal and Handforth. Along with other projects at the Styal Homes, the P.O.W.s helped in the construction of the new garden layout surrounding the new Church. The prisoners were paid seven pence per hour plus mid-day refreshment. One alarming incident brought fear to the villagers when it was disclosed that in 1915 one of the prisoners was in an advanced stage of Leprosy.

Though the War dominated the day-to-day events of the nation, it must be said that so far as the Cottage homes were concerned, 1915 is regarded as the year in which the Manchester Guardians came to Styal as the new Landlords of the 300 acre smallholding and also as the adopted parents of the 510 children of the Colony. Their takeover at Styal will always be a significant landmark in the history of Manchester and yet because of an unforeseen tragedy which occurred in the first month of office, all events of that year were tainted with despondency. Mr William Shaw, the well respected Superintendent and father figure of the Homes, died suddenly at his residence on Tuesday evening, May 6th. Once again the processes of mourning blanketed the Homes Colony, but if previous funerals had been considered a drama, the ensuing cortege was about to leave an imprint on the Styal landscape for many years to come. On the Saturday morning, on a day which bore all the hallmarks of beautiful Spring setting, the silent and orderly procession began its journey from the Superintendent's House, passing the growing foundations of the new church. From the gates of the institution the road to Styal village was lined on either side by all the children of the Homes. They stood with bowed heads like minature military sentinels as the coffin followed the muffled drumbeats of the uniformed Church Lads Brigade. The service at Northenden Parish Church of St Wilfred was filled to capacity, mainly by the children of Styal and the Manchester Regiment C.L.B. Apart from his immediate family, the numbers were made up from the staff of the Homes and all the top officials of the newly formed Manchester Guardians. During the service the Homes Band played the Dead March. At the final farewell at the family graveside, the buglers of the Gorton St. James Company of the C.L.B., sounded the Last Post.

During the next few months and years, the Manchester Guardians were to bring about many changes and improvements at the Homes which would benefit the children who were still living in an isolated environment and still no nearer to any form of social integration with the Greg's village colony. After many hundreds of applications for the post of Superintendent and Matron, the Guardians, in the interests of economy decided to let Mrs Shaw stay on at the Homes as the Superintendent. In so doing, there was a saving to the ratepayers of £200 per year and the Guardians could now escape any accusations of overspending at the Styal Cottage Homes. The old Mother and Father image dissappeared overnight as a new decade began for the children where law and order was handed on a plate to the House Mothers of each cottage. Styal Homes was now one of eleven institutions which were under the jurisdiction of the Manchester Guardians.

The headquarters of the Guardians at All Saints, served as the monthly meeting venue for all the various committees and sub committees which administered the various institutions. Under the grand title of; 'House Committee', they managed the affairs of the eleven establishments belonging to the all powerful Manchester Guardians including: New Bridge Street Institution, Withington Institution, Tame Street Institution, Crescent Road Inst., Delaunay's Road Institute, Booth Hall Infirmary, Styal Cottage Homes, Swinton Schools, Dr. Rhodes Memorial Home, Rose Hill Opthalmia School and Langho Epileptic Colony.

It was decided by the Guardians that the custom of training the girls at Styal for future emplyment in service should be continued and that a fixed wage of ten pounds per annum plus keep be recommended to would-be employers. For the boys who escaped the military calling an alternative had been found at the firm of Pilkington Brothers of St. Helens who, had recently requested the Manchester Guardians to supply boy apprentices. Other boys invariably made their way in life as agricultural workers in Cheshire. Like the girls, the boys were provided with a suit of clothing and their keep but in addition, they received twelve pounds per annum. Another innovation by the Guardians was to abandon the lettering and numbering of each cottage and substitute a name of a flower or tree. Thus 'A' Home, became Aster cottage and 'B' Home Begonia cottage and so on, through the alphabet. Perhaps the most touching gesture from the Boardroom was the one from Mr Jepson, who proposed that the two unmarked communal graves at Wilmslow Cemetery which had been purchased by the South Manchester Guardians in 1907 and 1913, should each be provided with a headstone. The oldest grave, which had been dug to a depth of 14 feet, contained ten coffins of young children, stacked on top of each other. Prior to 1907, the many children who died at the Homes, had been buried at Wilmslow Parish Church. Records of only five children in the pauper section of unmarked graves, can be seen and viewed at Wilmslow Parish Church.

At the year's end, over 500 children and staff crowded the Homes church for its first ever Christmas service. Many of the Guardians were present at this service, not only to celebrate the festive season but to display the 140 boxes of Comforts and Souvenir Book of the New Church building which were destined for the boys who were fighting at the front lines. The Rev. James, revealed that nine boys had already been killed in action and he hoped that the children present, would appreciate that they had died fighting for their future. At the close of the service, Mr Overmann the architect, presented a water colour drawing of the new Church to the Guardians, to be hung permanently in the Board Room.

The remaining three years of the Great War proved to be turbulent if not troublesome, at the Homes colony. Since the death of Mr Shaw and the departure of Mr Cochran, a moral decline had set in, which portrayed the frustrations of the boys and girls who were rebellious against the new petticoat system of law and order. 'Absconding' or 'Running Away' were now expressions adopted by Styal children for the rest of the duration. During this period, of unrest, a word which had been mentioned on more than one occasion, took root and was added to the vocabulary of Styal. To most of the children, 'prison' or 'Styal Prison' summed up the feelings of the orphans who were the victims of isolation from the outside world and who saw no future in the day to day existence of a Goldfish bowl. In an attempt to stem the tide of absconders, Mrs

Shaw enlisted the help of Mr Walker, her second in command, who, on a day in 1917, administered a public flogging as an example for future discipline. For those boys who persisted in running away from Styal, the answer now lay in deportation; not to foreign parts, but to a 'Training Ship' at the Navy League Sea Training Home, at Liscard, Birkenhead. More than twenty boys between the ages of thirteen and fifteen were enlisted on a training ship, due to their rebellious nature at the Home.

The village of Styal was now the major contributor of personnel for full or part time work at the Homes. In 1916 , a year which saw the emergence of the newly promoted Colonel Alex Greg, new faces and personalities were replacing the vacancies created by the tide of volunteers into the services. One such person was the portly Mr James Bone, the Baker• at the village Co-op Shop. His employment at the Homes was only made possible so long as Mrs Shaw's brougham could be used to transport him to and from the village every day, During May, an unexpected visitor arrived in the form of Pte. Alex Gradwell of the 181st Bn. of the Canadian Exp. Forces now in training at Brandon. He had left the village as a young man 16 years previously with his pal Walter Hope. Like many of the farmers and land workers of Canada, he informed his friends that he had given up his farm at Saskatchewan to come and fight the enemy in Europe. Also, he had called to see his mother's grave which he had been unable to do when she died a few months earlier. The next two years at the Homes revealed the identities of six more Canadian soldiers and former orphans of the Colony, on their way tothe War. One of those young soldiers was Alex Kingston Owen, an orphan who had left Styal at 12 years of age to work on a farm at Omemee, Ontario. Pte. 805763 Owen, of the C.E.F., called at Styal in 1917 but was never heard of again.

In the sweeping tide of militarism which was reaching out to every corner of Great Britain it was just a matter of time before the Homes of Styal became a prime target for Regiments of the realm. By the beginning of 1917, the Kings Royal Rifles Regiment had established a Cadet Corps which saw the end of the C.L.B. and the changeover to the khaki uniform of the K.R.R. One of three brothers and probably the first Homes boy to be enlisted in the K.R.R.s was David Hayes who, in his first year at the front lines was wounded. He was to make headline news in a Manchester newspaper the following year when, as a corporal, he received his second serious wounding in action, before his final departure to a Military hospital in

England. Band practice became secondary to the more pressing needs of regimented drill instruction at the Homes, so much so, that the boys dormitories resembled barrack rooms where uniforms and rifles - the old Boer War Rifle - were always to hand.

For only the second time in its 20 year history, a newspaper photographer came to the Homes Colony. The Wilmslow Advertiser recorded the occasion of 'A Visit from a V.C. Hero' - June 22nd, 1917. From this lengthy report, it appeared that the Guardians had conceived the idea of producing a real live V.C. for the benefit of the children and would-be soldiers of the Styal Cottage Homes. As the noonday train from Manchester pulled in to Styal station, the 42 strong squad of the Homes military band, burst into tune with the melody of "See the conquering hero comes". Together with the committee members of the Guardians, the special guest accompanied Mr Draper, the chairman, along Station Road where all the villagers had assembled en-masse to cheer him. At the Homes the younger children waved flags and formed a corridor for their hero to make his way on to the playing field and the specially prepared reception. At long last, Mr Draper introduced the uniformed soldier to the children. His name and title was Private George Stringer Manchester Regiment and, according to Mr Draper, had been the first Manchester born soldier to win the coveted Victoria Cross during the present conflict. After more speech making and a tour of the Homes, Pte. Stringer was presented with a bouquet by seven years old Lily Milton on behalf of all the children. Once more, the villagers of Styal waved to the 'hero' as he made his way to the station but before he left the village he was rewarded with a box of cigarettes by Mrs Royle who had made a collection on his behalf. At a later date in the year, the Homes band were to meet Pte. Stringer V.C. for a second time, at the Withington Institute where they were giving a concert at the Sports Day celebrations in aid of the war wounded.

At a committee meeting held in November 1916, the Manchester Guardians accepted a proposal from one of it's members, Mr T.M. Draper of 101 George Street, Moss Side, that a Girl Guide Company be formed for the benefit of the girls of the Homes. The motion was seconded by Miss Olga Hertz and in 1917 the newly formed Styal Company of the Girl Guides under the leadership of Captain Madge Greg, were the successful winners of a competition held on the day of the annual Sports and Parents Visiting Day. The 36 girls aged between 11 years and 15 years who formed the first Guide Troop, soon built a reputation as the best turned out Company in the district of Cheshire. The formation of the Girl Guides had succeeded in giving the girls of the Homes an identity which brought the same respect as the famous Boys Military Band and in a few short months, they were sharing the same platform and the same outings.

For the second time in two years, Mrs Shaw the Superintendent, wrote to the Guardians in Manchester, requesting them to pursue the release of Mr Cochran from his Regimental duties. Her second letter in 1918 coincided with the call up of Mr Walker Hinchcliffe, the acting Band Master and Drill Instructor. It was apparent that the under staffed and over crowded Homes were undergoing a period of trauma, when the returns for the first nine months of the year showed a total of 68 absconders, including some girls. Whether by accident or intention, it was significant that a letter from the Local Government Board should arrive at Mrs Shaw's house in her hour of need. During the summer months Mrs Shaw was asked to point out to the boys that there was a serious shortage of British seamen and also to tell them of the advantages to be gained from a course of training at a recognised Sea School. From this recruitment drive, 8 boys enlisted on the training ship Exmouth. Another 8 boys went to the Lancs Navy League Sea Training Home, Liscard, their ages ranging from 13 to 15 years, and another group of four boys joined the Royal Navy.

The Peace Treaty and the ending of the Great War on November 11th became the signal for the whole country to demonstrate its relief and jubilation. Styal was no exception in the display of mass hysteria which swept the landscapes of Europe. Again, each to his own, the Homes colony celebrated with a huge bonfire on the newly built cricket and football pitch which, ironically, had just been landscaped by the German P.O.W.s, whilst half a mile away the villagers repeated the same bonfire festivities on the Styal Cricket Green. In the forthcoming weeks and months the staggering costs in terms of human lives would be made known. Already the war casualty figures concerning the boy soldiers of the Homes had been revised for the third time. Finally, at the end of 1918, it was officially revealed that out of 179 boys who took part in the conflict, a total of 52 boys paid the penalty. Having obtained the necessary statistics, the Guardians requested Messrs J. Wippell & Co. Ltd, to provide two Oak Tablets for the Church. One would provide the names of those who served in the War and the other would give the names of the deceased. The agreed cost of the tablets, including the incised and gilded lettering was agreed at £35.12.6d and £45.0.0 for the roll of honour. To the relief of Mrs Shaw, the foreboding figure of Sgt Trumpeter John Cochran arrived home in April of 1919. Freshly equipped with his military experience and full of vigour and enthusiasm, he wasted no time in re-establishing the Homes Band as the leading military Band of the North West. The children who were newcomers to the Colony were about to witness the most ruthless form of discipline they had ever known, or would ever know. Following in the footsteps of Mr Cochran were many other ex-servicemen, now home from the wars. Amongst these 'old' soldiers were two of the teachers of the senior school. The first to arrive was Mr Deardon the assistant Headmaster whose term of office as a Poor Law Teacher at the Homes, ceased at the end of 1919 when he became the assistant Headmaster of Fulshaw School in neighbouring Wilmslow. Secondly, but by no means the last, came the young Mr Smith. He had volunteered in 1914 as a Private in the Cheshire Regiment and throughout the four yeas had been promoted to Corporal,Sergeant, Second Lieutenant and finally, Captain of the Quatermasters Stores.

Exactly six months after Mr Cochran's return, the Boys Military Band were back on the top rungs of the ladder of success by being the outstanding winners of the trophy awarded at the annual C.L.B. Camp at Lytham. Apart from a Cup, they shared a cash prize which went towards a day's outing at Belle Vue Pleasure Park. Three months later and again with Mr Cochran's influence, the Girl Guides of the Homes won a standard bearing Union Jack, as first prize for the best turned out, the best marching and the best drilled troop in the Stockport, Wilmslow and Alderley districts of Cheshire. The requests for the services of the Homes Band had become so numerous that some applications were turned down. It appeared that every township throughout the country was holding a 'Peace Day' rally during July and the Guardians had reserved the band's services for the Cottage Homes' own celebrations. On Saturday July 16th, the children marched behind the Band to Styal village where Capt. Madge Greg and the Girl Guide troop were assembled next to the Lurry Tableau, in readiness for the arrival of the Manchester Guardians. An indication that times had not changed was self evident. Just a few hundred yards from the Homes procession, the Oak School of the village, under Mr Bracegirdle the headmaster, was enacting it's own 'Peace Day' festival, around the Maypole on the Green and in the School room.

Vary rarely did the Children's Band enter the boundaries of Styal village and when they did, it was either by request or arrangement by the Greg family. One such occasion occured on Tuesday the 21st July 1919 when the society wedding of Emily Russell Greg of Lode Hill took place at the tiny Norcliffe Chapel. The selected band boys of the Homes, under the leadership of Mr Cochran, sounded the Wedding March as the bride walked down the red carpeted pathway and under a white canopy, arched between the flanking hedgerows. At the reception at Mr H.P. Greg's residence at Lode Hill, the Homes band continued the musical concert during the afternoon and evening.

In the eyes of the majority of the children of the Homes, the Band Boys were the elite of the colony, in that their duties took them away from the Institution not only on weekly outings but also to the annual camp at the seaside. For the two year period following the war, at a time when every urban district council and all manner of 'old comrades' associations were seeking finances for the erection of War Memorials, the Band were called upon no less than fifteen times. They were instrumental in collecting hundreds of pounds for Manchester and Cheshire War Memorials with the climax of their efforts being the invitation to perform at the unveiling ceremony at Manchester, Cheadle Hulme, Withington, Wilmslow and Styal. The local attendance and three of these extracts are as follows:-

"26th July 1920, the Styal Homes Military Band were allowed to play without a fee at the Laying of the War Memorial Stone at Cheadle Hulme."

"November 11th 1920, a special Armistice Service was held at Wilmslow Parish Church. The Wilmslow branch of the Comrades of the Great War attended. The Styal Homes Band led the service with the National Anthem and the Buglers sounded the Last Post at the conclusion. The Band was in attendance at both the morning and evening service when the Church was filled to capacity"

"Saturday 15th October 1921, the names of twenty four officers and men of Styal who made the supreme sacrifice in the late war are recorded upon the memorial which was unveiled by Col. E.W. Greg C.B.E. It was a unique ceremony, such as had never before been witnessed by the parish. Seating was provided directly in front of the monument and behind the chairs stood the hundreds of children from the Styal Cottage Homes together with the Girl Guides. The ex-servicemen of Styal and Handforth and the general public made up the masses of people who formed a large semi-circle accross the entrance of Station Road. The Styal Homes Band was accommodated on a platform on the corner of the roadway and on each side of the monument stood a firing party from Sandbach, belonging to the 7th Bn. The Cheshire Regt. Lt. Colonel Alex Greg presided. After the speeches which referred to the fallen lads of the village, Col. Ernest Greg pulled the sash of the national flag and unveiled the monument to the public gaze. After the echoes of the firing party had died away, the Last Post and Reveille was sounded by the Boys Band who ended the ceremony with several hymns. The memorial wall of the monument is of Alderley rustic stone and the whole of the work was carried out by N. and J. Mills of Wilmslow."

The final engagement of the band in connection with war memorials took place at Wilmslow on September 17th 1921. At this unveiling ceremony, the full troop of the Girl Guides and the Church Lad's Brigade were also on parade. Meanwhile, another trophy had been added to the Band's silverware collection when, on November 5th 1920, Major Grimshaw of the Kings Royal Rifle Cadet Corps, awarded the Styal Band, a silver mounted Drum Majors staff, in recognition of the Band's presentation and duties whilst at the annual camp. In stark contrast to the pomp and ceremony of all engagements in connection with war memorials, the Children's colony paid homage to their boy heros in a simple ceremony at the Church on 16th April 1921. The Guardians had announced the previous month, that the Bishop of Chester, after a Confirmation Service, would unveil the Roll of Honour to the 52 Boys of the Homes who had given their lives.

So much had happened in the military sense since the ending of the war, all other events had been overshadowed or reduced to a low profile. Quietly, but effectively, the wheels had been constantly in motion at the offices of the Guardians and many events had taken place which were to have an effect on the Styal landscape. One important issue which was to affect the day to day running of the Homes was the 1918 Act with regard to the Education and Employment of Children. Because the new Bill required children to spend an extra year at school until they were fifteen, the withdrawal of child labour had caused a serious staff shortage. With the consent of the Guardians, Mrs Shaw was permitted to advertise in the Wilmslow newspaper for ten additional Scrubbers and four Relief Housemothers. Yet another change at the Homes Oakwood Farm took place. Mr and Mrs Park were allowed to employ Miss Smith to help supervise the 20 boys who resided in the upstairs barn and an order was issued from the Manchester Committee that the practice of imbibing mid-day ale, was to cease, and that in future, tea only would be provided. To add to these changes of 1919, the Bishop of Chester was asked by the Guardians to nominate a new Chaplain for the Styal Homes, in the wake of the resignation of the Rev. James. In May of that year, the Rev H.J. Luxton was officially appointed from a church at Blackley. Since the acquisition of the Styal Colony, the Manchester Guardians had been constantly inundated with requests from all kinds of Woman's Unions and Guilds, to be allowed to visit the Homes as a Day Excursion. Eventually, permission was granted with the proviso that no more than twenty persons at one visit be allowed and that two weeks notice be given in advance. Mrs Shaw was instructed to give three days notice to the cottage which would receive the visitors and to inform the Guardians of any infectious diesease which were prevalent. With visitations being limited to weekdays only - whilst the children were at school - the first party to visit the Cheshire Homes was the Union of Co-operative Employees. They were the forerunners of hundreds of future visitors to the Homes over the next two decades and it was not unusual for the visitors to leave a donation towards a special fund for the children. By 1920 the demand by the various organisations to be allowed to visit the Colony on a day when they could meet and mingle with the children had become so overwhelming, the Guardians finally gave permission for parties of no more than twelve people at a time, to visit on a Saturday, between 2.0pm and 4.0pm.

If the Band was seen as being representative of the boys of Styal Homes, than equally, the ambassadors for the girls were the trained domestics who went into service. Their reputation for being above average, obedient and hard working, always ensured that applications were constantly ahead of supply. Hardly a week passed without a young domestic girl leaving the gates of the institution, bound for a post in the Cheshire area or a house in the Manchester suburbs. There has always been speculation about how many girls went into the employ of the Greg's of Styal but in the absence of early records, one can only guess. One instance of the Greg connection is the case of 16 year old Gladys Baker who, on the 19th November 1919, joined the other domestic servants at Norcliffe Hall. On that day, she was personally escorted by Mrs Shaw, who delivered her to the Norcliffe residence by brougham. Since Greg's Mill was not considered to be a place of employment with future prospects, boys from the Homes were discouraged from becoming apprenticed.

However, history records that one Ernest Gilham, aged 16 years, entered the service of Greg Bros, in 1922 to learn weaving. Mabel Fay, who was a senior Girl Guide and friend of Gladys Baker, went into service with Mr Overmann, the well known Architect of Didsbury. By the year 1921, the guardians had not only reviewed the wages paid to the boys and girls, but recommended that in future the boys on the farms were to be paid £26 per year, whilst the girls were to receive £17 per year. Canada and the unsavoury memories of child deporatation, were renewed briefly when in 1921, Mr Arthur Nicholson of St Catherine's Ontario, wrote to the Manchester Guardians requesting them to let him have a boy from Styal to look after his motor car and a girl to serve as a domestic servant. After a discussion with the House Committee, a reply was forwarded to Canada, informing Mr Nicholson that there was no boy or girl available. It was evident that the Guardians wished to wipe their hands of the taint of child emigration, for during the following month, the Homes were trying to cope with a surplus of boys who were 16 years of age. To relieve themselves of the burden, an advertisement was placed in the Manchester papers, inviting applications for their services.

The great influenza epidemic of 1921, a legacy of the Great War,became an unwelcome visitor to Styal as it was to most of the British Isles. The already isolated children of the colony became virtual prisoners of circumstances. Visits in and out of the colony were limited for almost twelve months and the services of the Band were jeopardised accordingly. Out of the seemingly depressed period, a ray of sunshine came in the form of a secondhand cinematograph machine which the Guardians purchased. They also hired films to be shown every fortnight, at a cost of two pounds ten shillings per evening, from Mrs Laski, a member of the Guardians and also of the Laski Film Company. In terms of progress, a futuristic event took place at the school in 1921. For the first time in its history, the senior school were allowed to submit the names of boys and girls who were considered to be capable of winning a scholarship to the Manchester Schools of Higher Education. The results of this foray were that three boys and three girls obtained places at Ducie Avenue Central School and two boys, John Atherton and John W Taylor, gained free admission to the Central high School, Whitworth Street, Manchester. So that the Guardians could discharge their obligations for the welfare of the children, these and all the subsequent scholarship children, were housed at Dr Rhodes Memorial Home, Didsbury. Mr Thomas Draper, the newly elected chiarman of the

Styal Homes Committee, was to set a precedent in 1921 when, at his suggestion, the other Guardians adopted his ideas and agreed to promote a spirit of competitiveness amongst the children of the colony. The outcome of this scheme was the presentation by Mr Draper of a silver cup, to be awarded to the boy who best merits it for a), excellence in school work and b), general conduct and behaviour in the Homes. The cup was to be known as the 'Draper Cup' and would be competed for on an annual basis. At the annual Sports Day in 1922, Mr Blackwell commented in his School Log: "Mr Draper awarded a cup to be known as the 'Draper Cup' to the best boy who best merits it for educational progress in school and for conduct generally - reports to be furnished by the Superintendant and Chaplain. The Cup to be held for twelve months" By 1923 some committee members who had compaigned for girls to be included in the Draper Cup scheme, were presented at the Sports Day in August. Again, Mr Blackwell made a note of the occasion and duly wrote in his log book: "In conjunction with the Superintendent and Chaplain, I recommend Charles Slater and Lily banks as the first holders of the Draper Cups to be presented in August. I look upon this as the most interesting event in connection with Education, during the whole of my 25 years at Styal". Along with the Cup, a silver medal bearing the inscribed name and date was awarded to the winners of the coveted prize. During the ensuing years up to 1927, the 'Draper Cup' was awarded to:-

Alice Gaulton - Fred Williams	1924
Alice Carr - Eric Thompson	1925
May Flower - Harold Slater	1926

Chapter 11

'THE NORCLIFFE SAGA'

History has been known to repeat itself in world affairs and in the social and economic growth of a nation. Very rarely does this phenomenon take place within a span of a quarter of a centry and the odds against such an event happening in a tiny village hamlet must be astronomical. Yet the date of Wednesday the 16th June 1920 will go down in history as a day the Greg's of Styal would wish to forget. In all probability the initial sequence of events began on 6th May 1920 when the death was announced of Mrs Margaret Greg widow of Mr R Greg (MP) of Bolton and Styal. For the next few weeks, there appeared to be a lull in the ensuing drama and yet in another sense, the village was making its own historical progress. A local man and former employee of Quarry Bank Mill, Mr Harry Earlam opened the doors of the Styal Post Office for the first time in March 1920. The building, opposite the Ship Inn had amongst other projects been used as a Coal Merchants. Originally it had begun life as a Store and Stables for the Ship Inn Brewery business. Records of this building only date back to 1874 when Mr Walter Walton, the host of the Old Ship Inn passed away. His epitaph included a mention of his brewer Mr Thomas Radcliff, and the stables opposite which were home to the carthorses. A few yards down Altrincham Road, PC Bendall was taking leave of the Police House and saying his farewells after nine years at Styal. About the time Harry Earlam began his Post Office and Sweets and Cigarettes business, a big celebration took place at the Village Club rooms at the Ship Inn. The occasion was the award of Cups to ex Servicemen but more especially to applaud the recent investiture by the King to Col. Ernest Greg C.B. and Col. Alex Greg C.B.E. Once again and for the last time, Alex Gradwell the old Styal boy and now a member of the 44th Bn of the Canadian Forces, called at the village with his fiancee Nurse Mason, of Westmorland. He informed the villagers that he would be marrying Miss Mason in May at Winnipeg.

In order to portray the episode of Norcliffe and its unfolding revelations one has only to study the chronology of the minutes of the Manchester Guardians which begin thus:-

25th February 1920 Letter from the Styal Homes Sub Committee to the board of Guardians.

"It has recently come to the knowledge of the Members of the Styal Committee that the portion of the estate of Mr Greg of Styal on the other side of the main road leading to the Cottage Homes is about to be sold. As it has for a long time been felt that if this land could be purchased by the Guardians it would be a most valuable acquisition for Milk producing purposes and for any development which may be required in the future of the Styal Cottage Homes, the Committee caused enquiries to be made by an agent, who has ascertained that the owner of the land will only sell to same by public auction. It appears that three farms are to be sold, comprising altogether about 350 acres. The farms may however, be sold separately. The agent has not yet been able to obtain the necessary details regarding the sale to enable a valuation to be made, but he hopes to have this information shortly. It is desired to have the opinion of the Board as to whether they would authorise the Styal Committee to purchase at a public auction one or more of the farms referred to after obtaining a valuation. Unless the shortness of notice of the sale prevents it, the Guardians will be given a further opportunity of stating whether they desire the purchase to be made after obtaining fuller particulars".

19th May 1920

'It was decided that a Sub Committee consisting of Messrs Reynolds, Barratt, Dook, Draper, Pendlebury, be appointed to carry out any necessary negotiations in connection with the proposed purchase of three Farms, situate on the opposite side of the main road to the Cottage Homes, which are about to be sold by auction'

2nd June 1920 Letter from the Manchester Guardians to the Ministry of Health, London.

"I am directed by the Guardians of this Union to make application for the sanction of the Ministry to their proposal to purchase at a Public Auction the following Farms situate in the immediate vicinity of the Guardians Cottage Homes and Estate at Styal, Cheshire, for sums not exceeding the amounts named.

Lot 1.	Norcliffe Farm	71½ acres	£7,000
Lot 2.	Cross Farm	26 acres	£3,500
Lot 3.	Oak Farm	80 acres	£7,500

In support of the application I am requested to state that the Guardians are desirous of securing the above farms for the following reasons, - firstly, for the production of pure milk for consumption by the patients in the Guardian's Hospitals: secondly, to have available the most suitable site should the Guardians or their successors at any time in the future find it necessary or desirable to extend the Cottage Homes at Styal: thirdly, to remove the possibility of the land fronting the road separating Norcliffe and Cross Farms from the Guardians' estate being used by others for building purposes.

I may say that the Farms could be worked without difficulty as they are only separated from the Guardians Farm at Styal by the road leading to the Homes. The Farms are situated close to the Station at Styal.

I may add that the Guardians are most anxious not to lose the opportunity if the prices are reasonable of purchasing these farms, particularly Norcliffe and Cross Farms, and they consider, in view of the situation and richness of the land, that they will be a most valuable acquisition to themselves and their successors and to Manchester.

The Guardians comtemplate shortly, subject to the permission of the Ministry of Health, selling their New Bridge Street property and if the Ministry is willing to sanction to the present proposal the Guardians would suggest that the portion of the proceeds from the sales of the New Bridge Street premises should be utilised towards defraying the proposed expenditure.

Having regard to the date of the sale by Public Auction vis. the 16th inst, the Guardians are anxious to receive an early reply to their application".

10th June 1920 or thereabouts -
The Ministry of Health informed the Guardians that having considered all the evidence they would only agree to the purchase of Norcliffe Farm and at a price not exceeding £7,000.

11th June 1920 - at the Railway Hotel, Wilmslow, at 4.0pm

'Sale of STYAL ESTATE Cheshire':

Lot 1, - All that Valuable Freehold Dairy and Produce Growing

Farm know as Norcliffe Farm Styal, now in the occupation of Mr Gleave, and containing 71 ½ acres or thereabouts.
Lot 2, - All that Freehold Farm or Small Holding known as Cross Farm Styal, now in the occupation of Mr Henry Hope, and containing 26 acres or thereabouts.
Lot 3 - All that well known Freehold Dairy and Produce Growing Farm known as the OAK FARM Styal, now in the occupation of Mr George Gardner and containing 80 acres or thereabouts.

18th June 1920 - The Wilmslow Advertiser

"The Styal Estate was sold by Sam D Walton at the Railway Hotel on Wednesday night. There was big crowd and remarkable bidding for this old estate of Mr R Greg former M.P. for Manchester, one of the oldest estates in Cheshire. All lots were quickly sold at high prices. The results included Oak Farm £6,000. Norcliffe Farm, £5,100. Cross Farm £2,700. There were an additional eight Lots in the Sale".

21st July 1920 - Minutes of meeting of the Manchester Guardians

"After hearing reports of the Styal Homes Sub Committee, regarding the sale of the 3 Farms opposite the Cottage Homes, it was decided to approve the action of the Deputy Clerk along with Mr Larmuth the valuer, the purchasing of the Norcliffe Farm, for the sum of £5,100.

May - August 1921

Between the above dates, Colonel Greg of Norcliffe Hall, wrote a series of letters to the Manchester Board of Guardians indicating that he would like to buy the Boundary land between Norcliffe Farm and Cross Farm and also indicated that he would like to acquire the Norcliffe Farm.

September 1921 - Meeting of the Styal Homes Sub Committee and the Board of Guardians -

After receiving Colonel Greg's final letter which asked them to consider his offer to purchase Norcliffe Farm, it was decided that Col. Greg be informed that the Guardians had no desire to sell the Farm. However, in reply to another request from Col. Alex Greg, it was decided that Col. Greg be allowed to have the shooting rights over Norcliffe Farm at a rental of £5 per annum.

The disclosure of these facts should now dispel the rumours and speculation which have plagued Styal and Manchester for the past 50 years. Most people and some historians have always linked the missing Norcliffe Farm from the Quarry Bank Estate with the death of Thomas Tylston Greg on September 18th 1920, at the Coles Estate in Hertfordshire. What is more feasible is the less popular story which tells of a farcical mix up between the agents of the Greg's and the Guardians at the Styal Estate Land sale. Whatever the reasons, the Greg's of Styal had once again been foiled by the Board of Guardians in almost identical circumstances. Whether the loss of Norcliffe Farm caused any ill feeling between the two factions, one can only surmise. On the other hand, the incident did nothing to heal the long standing enmity between the two landlords of Styal and if anything, the possible merger of the two colonies had taken a backward step.

THE INDUSTRIAL SCHOOLS, SWINTON.

SWINTON SCHOOLS.

Chapter 12

'THE PALACE PAUPERS'

Like the ticking of a clock, the hours, the days and the weeks were approaching the count-down to the year of 1924, a year which was to undergo major change at both the colonies of Styal. The Homes Military Band was will notching success upon success, so much so, that it became synonymous with, 'another year - another trophy'. In 1924 the Colonel Commandant of the Church Lads Brigade made a special request to the Guardians for - 'permission for the Styal Homes Compy of the C.L.B. to form a Guard of Honour for the visit to Manchester of Lord Methuen (Field Marshal) During the annual Camp at Rhyl in 1923 the Band and cadets of the K.R.R. was awarded the coveted Darlington Shield for all round efficiency. A more important and meaningful engagement for the Band's services occured on 29th September 1922 when the Guardians proudly showed the child ambassadors to the ordinary people of Manchester. Officially the occasion had been advertised as "The Unveiling Ceremony and Reunion of the Crumpsall Nurses" It was a day which belonged to the Guardians; the VIPs and all their employees, past and present. Not only was a memorial tablet with the inscribed names of all former nurses of the Infirmary unveiled but also a bust of the famous Edith Cavell. A grand patriotic concert by the Homes Band accompanied the day's proceedings.

Mr Morley an official Government Inspector of Schools paid a brief and unexpected visit to the Styal Homes Schools during the Spring of 1923. His report to the Guardians highlighted a deficiency in the colony system which was apparent and well known by the serving Poor Law Teachers. His summing up of the situation at Styal took just one sentence :- "In a school of this kind, two special points are worthy of attention a) the children are severley lacking in initiative and b) their speech is barely audible and most indistinct." Not surprising the teachers replied to H M Inspector that more could and should be done to improve the elocution amongst the children and took great pains to point out that the malady was unique to the institutional system at Styal. They concluded their report : - "progress is very slow probably owing in some measure to the rare opportunities afforded to the children in coming into contact and conversing with outside people and situations". Following the visit of the Schools Inspector the school-leaving age was lowered to 14 years and in consequence of this ruling the girls who were eligible continued a two year training in Domestic Housewifery. Various trades were available to the boys but by far the majority were placed on the Homes Oakwood Farm to be taught a three year course of scientific farming by the experienced Mr Park. In retrospect 1923 proved to be disastrous for the college trained Farm Bailiff. Mrs Park the former Homes Nurse and wife of six years, died suddenly on October 7th. No sooner had the grieving Mr Park returned to normal duties when out of the blue tragedy struck again. In November, his farm was declared 'out of bounds' due to an outbreak of Foot and Mouth disease which resulted in the mass slaughter of many of the animals. Again a few months later the dreaded swine fever struck and the entire herd of 50 Pigs was put down. Because of the disruption to the milk supply to the Homes, the Guardians waived the contract which Mr Gleave of Norcliffe Farm had been awarded and he was requested to supply the necessary milk to the Homes instead of the Manchester Institutions.

A day in late July of 1923 when all the officers of the Manchester 6th Btn of the Manchester Regiment of the Church Lads Brigade assembled at the Styal Homes for a field day would normally pass without formality. It was after all, just another gathering of the Bandboys and Cadets, an occasion which was quite common to the children of the Colony. Had it not been for the revelations in connection with the former boys of the Homes, July 18th, would have become inconspicuous in the diary of Manchester Guardians. As it was, the boys learned something about the former history of the Brigade and of the part which Styal Homes had contributed. The Commandant, after his introductory speech about the objects of the Church Lads Brigade which included 'the advancement of Christ's Kingdom among lads of all classes of the Church of England, the promotion of reverence, discipline, self respect, and all that tends towards true Christian manliness, Motto: "Fight The Good Fight", continued: 'The C.L.B. joined together with the Empire Cadet movement in 1911 which in turn, gave the Brigade its Territorial Army Association. The annual Camps. usually held at Prestatyn, contained up to 3,000 Cadets. At the onset of the Great War, Field Marshall Lord Grenfell, Governor and Commandant, placed the whole of the organisation at the disposal of the War Office. At that time, there were 20,000 cadets who were accepted by the Government although only half of that number were 17 years of age and eligible for service. On the proposal and recommendations of Lord Grenfell, permission was granted by the War Office for a formation of a Special Battalion, to be identified with the Church Lad's Brigade. By the 5th September 1914, the Headquarters of the C.L.B. received the expected confirmation of the War Office which also thanked the movement for their patriotic offer. Under the influence of Lord Grenfell, a battalion of former and present serving members of the C.L.B. formed part of the Kings Royal Rifles and became known as the 16th Bn, Kings Royal Rifles. The village of Denham in Buckinghamshire became the Camp Headquarters and by the end of the year, the young soldiers were in the trenches. During 1917 the whole of the C.L.B. movement throughout the country were issued with a change of uniform and exchanged the blue C.L.B. for the khaki K.R.R. Cadet issue. Many more facts about the past history of the Brigade were revealed during the speechmaking but with regard to the Styal Homes Boys, it was said "a good representation had been made by the boys of the Styal Company of the C.L.B. during the Great War".

The Centenary of Norcliffe Chapel was highlighted for most of the year, both by the newspaper articles and the celebrations at the village, for this was the year of 1924, a year when the whole village seemed to be dominated by change and circumstances. In the shadow of the Norcliffe festivities, 'The Brave Captain'- Col Alex Greg was saying his farewells to his family and friends prior to his final departure from his beloved Styal. He had already requested the Manchester Guardians to allow him to transfer the 'shooting rights' of Norcliffe Farm, to his brother, Col. Ernest to which the Board had agreed. Colonel Greg's departure to the South of England was an indication of the downward spiral of the once famous Quarry Bank Empire which by now, was in a state of decline from which it would never recover. John Cochran - Junior - the eldest son of the Homes Bandmaster, handed his resignation to the Board of Guardians and informed them that he was emigrating to Canada. He had spent fourteen years at Styal and was a musician at both colonies. At one time, he was a member of the Styal String Orchestra, but more prominently a Bandsman of the C.L.B. Mr Cochran encouraged his son to emigrate to Canada with the intention that he himself would follow in a couple of year's time.

"RETIREMENT OF MRS MARY KATE SHAW" - 'Superintendent who mothered 9,500 Chidren' -

'Unbroken Association with Styal Cottage Homes'. Each of these proclamations by the local Advertiser newspaper on July the 4th, confirmed the rumours which had been circulating in the Colony since April, when Mrs Shaw declared her intentions to the Guardians. The news was broken to the children and staff of the Homes on the day on which the Gala and Parents visiting day took place. Amongst the usual visitors on the Wednesday Sports Day were the Committee members and wives etc., and also the children from Buckley Hall, Rochdale and Holly Mount, Bury. Throughout the day the accolades to Mrs Shaw were falling like confetti, not least those from the serving members of the Styal Committee. The Brother Superior of Buckley Hall, Brother Ramon, paid a glowing tribute to Mrs Shaw, as did Mr. Geraghty who spoke on behalf of the Mother Superior of Holly Mount. It was without doubt the duty of the Chairman of the Guardians to have the final say and pay the final tribute to an extra ordinary Mother of 25 years standing. Mr Draper responded to the challenge by referring to the quality of the work undertaken by Mrs Shaw and the progress in Child Welfare during the first quarter of the century. In summing up the life and work of the Superintendent, Mr Draper's last comments were an adaptation of Shakespeare's words "Her life was gentle, and the elements so mixed in her, that Nature might stand up, and say to all the world - this was a Woman!" Although Mrs Shaw was ailing in health, she agreed to stay on at the Homes until the committee had decided upon her successor.

So far as the Guardians were concerned, the timing of Mrs Shaw's retirement could not have been better. A crucial meeting had recently taken place, to consider the future of the Poor Law Children as a whole in the Manchester area and the mounting costs to the ratepayers. The subject which had given the Guardians most concern and which had needed government approval was the proposed closure of the Swinton Industrial Schools, Chorley Road, Swinton. This old Victorian Institution which had been built by the Manchester Guardians in 1843, was a monumental three tier 'barrack system' building which was home to 1,000 children at a time. Ever since Charles Dickens had paid a visit to the Institution and had likened it to "a Palace for the Pauper children" it, and its inmates had assumed the nickname of 'Palace Paupers'. The only hiccup had been the question of the future segregation of the Roman Catholic children from the Church of England children and their future destination. On the 16th July, at the All Saints Boardroom, Mr Draper and his sub committee, proposed the following agenda which was accepted and approved by the Guardians:-

"The committee considered matters relating to the Homes in consequence of the closing of Swinton Schools, and also filling the vacancy caused through the resignation of Mrs Shaw, and decided to recommend to the Styal Homes Committee :-

(1) That 12 additional Homes be erected on the Styal Estate to accommodate about 180 children.

(2) That additional school accommodation be provided - the type, to be decided at a future meeting of the sub committee.

(3) That Mr F.H. Overmann, F.M.S.A. be requested to prepare plans.

(4) That Mr and Mrs A.J. Blythe, Master and Head Schoolmaster, and Matron respectively of the Swinton Schools, be appointed Superintendent and Matron respectively at the Styal Cottage Homes, it being understood and accepted :-

(a) That Mr Blythe will also be appointed as Head Master of the Schools at Styal when a vacancy occurs in that office.

(b) That Mr and Mrs Blythe will continue to act as Master and Head Schoolmaster, and Matron of the Swinton Schools until such schools are closed, and,

(c) That Mr and Mrs Blythe be paid at their present rate of remuneration, such remuneration to be apportioned between the two establishements.

(d) That Mr Blythe commence duties as Superintendent of Styal Cottage Homes on 1st October.

If ever an opportunity had presented itself for the children of Styal to be integrated into the 20th century under a new system and under the influence of a futuristic young Superintendent and Matron at the helm, this was that moment. There can be no doubt that Mr and Mrs Blythe won the day on the grounds of economy, and the Guardians had claimed a strategic victory. Not only had Mr and Mrs Blythe saved the ratepayers a three year salary of a Superintendent and Matron at Styal, but the claim by Mr Blythe for the headmastership would not necessitate expenses of a salaried Headmaster at a future date.

Mr Blythe apart from two court appearances for excessive caning, had an exemplary record for past services as Superintendent and Headmaster at Swinton. His 56 years in age did not deter the Guardians who considered his fourteen years experience at Swinton, to be of apt compensation. Prior to 1910 he had held a similar post as Superintendent and Headmaster at St Mary's School, under the Islington Board of Guardians, a post which lasted six years. As a young man with a college degree, he commenced his career with the South Metropolitan District School at Sutton, Surrey, where he was assistant Headmaster to nearly 3,000 children. Like most parents, Mr and Mrs Blythe had suffered the loss of two sons during the Great War, one of whom, a former pupil of Chethams School, had been awarded the Military Cross whilst serving with the Manchester Regiment. By the Christmastime of 1924 Mr Blythe had made his presence known at the Styal colony by implementing two major changes to the curriculum. Firstly, with the permission of the Guardians he requested that the children of each cottage from the age of 7 years and upwards, be given more work schedules to make up for staff shortages. Secondly, that the children at the senior school should salute the Headmaster on entering the school each day. Another ruling over the Christmas period had been implemented as a result of a suggestion by Mr Draper. 'The committee decided that each cottage at Styal Homes should have an individual party of its own so that children can invite their friends from other cottages and as a result of this decision, brothers and sisters will have the opportunity of being re-united.'

When the first foothold had been gained at Styal in 1894 it was , according to the newspapers "The Year of the Water". If comparisons could be made between 1894 and 1927 - the year the 'palace paupers' came to Styal - a more appropriate title to 1927 would be: 'The Year of the Floods'. After a promising Springtime, the Summer and Autumn were to go down on record - according to Manchester newspaper - as, "The Worst Summer For Years". The second half of 1927 was catalogued in most newspapers and some of the captions in reference to the appalling weather conditions, read like a page of Noah's Diary. - "Colds and Influenza epidemic predicted after the lack of any Summer weather" - "Blackpool under 30 foot waves and sand everywhere" - "Morecambe Pier breaks in two" - "Snow falls in East Cheshire during September" - "Submerged Train Driver rescued by Driver at Fleetwood" - "Disaster Fund for Flood Victims of Fleetwood, six people drowned and many missing" - "In Manchester, parts of Platt Fields are under two feet of water". Amidst this watery background, the 180 children arrived at Styal during the first week of September to take up residence in the six new homes which had been built on the site between the existing Homes and Oakwood Farm. Meanwhile, the remaining 200 Roman Catholic children of the Swinton schools were separated, the boys going to Buckley Hall and the girls to Holly Mount. Many of the staff and teachers of Swinton, joined the children at their new place of Institution and in the case of the Styal immigrants, no less than six school teachers accompanied the children. Their names were listed as: Mr Watson, Mrs Frazer, Miss Howatt, Miss Coleman, Miss Bedford, and Mr Dutton. Also listed, was the arrival of Miss Hasmun, a long serving member of the Swinton Institution and a former Matron of one of the 100 bed Dormitories. Her future role at Styal was to be Assistant Matron. Unfortunately. the reign of Mr Dutton was short lived, for in 1928, whilst refereeing a football match at the Homes, he literally dropped dead. Unlike former occasions of importance to the Guardians, the opening ceremony of the new homes became a mere formality. For one reason or another the planned schedule for the 14th September, failed to materialise and a delayed opening was arranged two days later on Friday 16th, at which time the Schools were closed to enable the Styal children to give their support to the occasion. As a token to commemorate another historic achievement by the guardians, a silver medallion was issued to every child of the Styal Cottage Homes, bearing the inscription 'Presented by T.M. Draper, Chairman, 14th September 1928 - Opening of Extensions to Styal Homes'.

Mr Cochran's planned retirement to Canada received a setback when the Guardians requested him to stay at the homes as Bandmaster and Drill Instructor. He was, in the opinion of the Committee, the best man for the job and accordingly, would be awarded an increase in salary. However, one departure which could not be prevented, was that of Mr Blackwell, Headmaster since 1898 and the most respected member of the community. His retirement cleared the way for Mr Blythe to commence duties as his successor on November 1st 1927. The figure of Mr F.V. Smith still hovered in the wings, waiting, as it were, for future advancement from Assistant Headmaster, but the time was not yet. In retrospect, the Homes and the children were to benefit from the progressive policies of Mr Blythe's term of office but unfortunately, his brand of progress did not come cheaply. Mr Blythe's institutionalism, Mr Cochran's Sergeant Major 'militarism and Mr Smith's school discipline formed a trio which spelled fear for years to come. From the names put forward as contestants for the Draper Cup awarded in 1927, the eventual winners of the Silver medal were Herbert Bickerton who at 12 years of age, was the leading Cornet player of the Band, and Mary Spencer aged 11. If ever a Styal Homes girl deserved a medal for courage and achievement, Mary Spencer was that girl. As a foundling, she had survived her first delicate years at Dr Rhodes' Home before her transfer to Styal. Like most of her counterparts she passed from year to year without a birthday or a visit from any relative, slowly and methodically yielding to the inevitable institutionalism. By the following year, she had not only excelled as the most promising pupil at the Senior School but along with five other children, won a scholarship to the Manchester Central High School. With a future full of promise Mary Spencer returned to Manchester to take up residence in the former Dr Rhodes' Home which had been converted into a Hostel for Scholarship winners from Styal. After four years of what seemed to be the best years of her life and with a Birthday on Christmas Day which had been awarded to her by her many friends from Styal, Mary Spencer died. Her death was the cause of great sorrow at the Rhodes Home and yet, during her high fever and maybe a premonition of her fate, she was able to will her only possession - the Draper Medal - to her best friend. In accordance with the rules and regulations, Mary Spencer was buried in a communal pauper grave at Phillips Park Cemetary on 20th October 1932.

One more change to the village landscape concluded the year of 1927. The seemingly insignificant obituary of Mr J H Henshall which appeared in the Advertiser on September 9th, not only served as a reminder of the long standing role of the Henshall's as the Village Smithy, but highlighted what was to become known as the end of an era and, the last village blacksmith. The Manchester Guardians, on whose land now stood the empty cottage and Smithy, placed an advertisement in the Evening News during November, which read 'To Let; Corner of Styal Road and Sagars Road' Out of a virtual flood of applicants and months of indecision and speculation, the new tenant was announced as Mr Jones, a former employee of Col. Greg who proposed changing the old Smithy into a Garage and a Gasoline Station. From that time until now, the old cottages and Garage - now updated - still form a part of the original landscape.

Never in the history of the Styal Homes had so much excitement been generated by the children of every age group. Mr Blythe, in his announcement that from 1928 onwards, there would be a two week holiday at the seaside, had become an overnight hero. Apart from the Bandboys and the Cadets who attended a two week Camp every year, no child from Styal had ever known a holiday as such. What was not general knowledge was the fact that the large bell tents had been used by the Swinton Schools children under Mr Blythe, for the past 14 years, for an annual 4 week holiday on the Lancashire coast. The Swinton Schools holiday excursion had been a concession from the Manchester Guardians only because of the determination of their Superintendent. Perhaps if Mr Shaw had lived, perhaps if Styal had not been so isolated; perhaps if the accusations against the Guardians for overspending at Styal had not been overpublicised, then maybe the children of Styal Homes might have benefited from the same opportunities as other institutions. Following behind the Band formation and its fanfare of military music, the marching feet of hundreds of children spilled out of the gates of the Homes onto Styal Road where they set off for the village station. Every mature boy and girl had undergone a drill rehearsal on the playing fields of the colony on how to ascend and descend from a train and now the big day had arrived when Mr Cochran would give the order for the children to board the special excursion train, bound for Squares Gate, Blackpool.

In terms of importance, the Homes Band of 1928 is worthy of yet another mention, for not only was this the year that all military links were severed with the Kings Royal Rifle Regt. but the old blue uniform of the C.L.B. battalions from all over the country had gathered in Hyde Park, London, and Mr Cochran and the Styal company were requested to provide the musical interlude during the inspection. For Mr Cochran the pomp and ceremony of the day was by no means at an end. Sometime during the proceedings the uniformed Mr Cochran, his tunic emblazoned with medals, was introduced and shook hands with King George V, and the Prince of Wales. At a later day during October, the Belle Vue Sports Stadium in Manchester, staged on exhibition which again involved the Homes Cadets. Outlined in a Manchester newspaper, the caption read: 'Styal Homes C.L.B. chosen to perform duties of Guard of Honour to Prince Arthur Duke of Cannaught'. One of the major traditions of the Homes was the leading role played by the 1st Cornetist of the Band. Ever since Mr Cochran had arrived at Styal, he had established a tradition based on his military background. Each morning, apart from weekends, the trumpet player would march to a central point of the colony and in true military fashion, sound the Revellie as a signal for the children to start the day, Similarly, at seven or eight o'clock in the evening, the same bugler would sound the Last Post as a signal for lights out and bedtime. During 1928 Mr Cochran discontinued his links with the Styal Village Club as a serving musician and organised a small but enterprising Band of his own, mainly for functions in the Wilmslow area.

On February 27th 1929, six children of the Homes were escorted to Manchester by Mrs Frazer to sit their exam for a scholarship award. A short time after their departure, Mr Draper of the Guardians arrived in the company of a uniformed military man of some importance. He was, according to Mr Draper, interested in boys who would like to make a career as Army Bandsmen. At a later date it was disclosed that the distinguished looking Captain held more than a passing interest in the Homes. Bandmaster A.M. Grice of the 2nd Durham Light Infantry had been a former boy of the colony and his admission number, when the Homes had first opened, was No. 4. The Superintendent of the Homes suffered a personal loss when his wife died at the colony during October. A memorial service to the late Mrs Blythe was held on 24th October, when over 600 children and staff of the Homes attended. At 60 years of age, Mr Blythe had great cause to be concerned about his future. He was aware of the circulating rumours amongst the Guardians about future changes at Styal and also of the threat to the establishment of the Manchester Guardians. Another indication of the approaching phase, came with the visit to Styal Homes on February 7th, of a deputation from the Manchester Education Committee, headed by Miss Kingsmill Jones. Six weeks later an entry of some importance was written into the Log Book of the Homes which read : 'March 21st, Today is the last occasion on which the Committee will meet at Styal Homes. The whole of the children were assembled in front of the Board Room at 2.30pm in order that the Guardians may see the children for the last official occasion. Miss Olga Hertz presented the Cup to the Band, which they had won in the Brigade. The two Draper Cup award nominees were Joseph Rochford and Mary Cummings'.

On April Fool's Day 1930, the children of Styal Homes exchanged parentage for the third time in the history of the Colony and were now the wards of Manchester Education Committee, a subsidary of the Public Assistance Committee administration. The Local Government Act on the 31st March, had finally brought to an end the reign of Boards of Guardians and all that they stood for. In reference to Styal and the Institution, the M.E.C. listed the assets as following:- 'The Institution in the 300 acre estate at Styal consists of 36 houses, a place of worship, 2 schools, 1 Hospital, Recreation Hall, Bandroom, Workshops, Sports Field, Superintendants quarters, Oakwood Farm and allotments. In addition the estate contains a second farm - Norcliffe - let for private farming. Nine cottages for employees. There are 415 children in residence but accommodation is available for 629 children. Also in residence, a staff of 71 Housemothers and assistants'. Ten years after this the Public Assistance Committee was to take on another title, that of 'Social Welfare Committee'. The expected retirement of Mr Blythe came on 7th September 1933. His entry in the Log Book was brief and to the point : "I am retiring from the position of Headship of these schools today. This is my last entry. signed: Blythe". After a retirement presentation was made to him by the two head pupils, Mr Blythe gave a farewell speech in which he referred to the year of 1931. He was justly proud of the Homes school that year when a record of 17 children passed the scholarship exams for the Manchester schools.

After a spate of advertising and a record entry of applicants during the year, the M.E.C. decided in favour of Mr and Mrs Higgins as the new Superintendent and Matron of the Homes. In true military fashion, Mr Cochran organised a reception for his future employer by parading all his young Bandboys and Cadets for an inspection march past. At this introductory ceremony the timid boys and girls of the Homes gazed in awe at the giant figure of their Superintendent. Mr Edwin John Higgins, formerly of the Ongar Homes at Chelmsford, Essex and an ex-lieutenant of the Lancashire Fusiliers during the Great War, was still a young man at 37 years of age. His imposing height of well over six foot together with a large framed physique did nothing to ease the anxieties of the children and yet, at that first meeting, there was something about the tall handsome military figure, which gave a glimmer of hope in a colony which was still locked in the Victorian era and still abiding by the old fashioned rules of institutionalism.

Like their predecessors, Mr and Mrs Higgins were about to enjoy a status at Styal Homes which had no equal in any other establishment of the Manchester Education Committee. True, they had a position of great responsibility and were answerable to their superiors but, by way of compensation their lifestyle was luxurious. From day one, the Homes, under the Guardians had produced a constant flow of female labour, trained to a high standard of domesticity. Whether it was a 'Upstairs Maid', 'Downstairs Maid', 'Between Maid', 'Maid of all

Work', Styal had provided all these, including 'Dairy Maids' and 'Farm Servants'. During the final year of domestic training, it became the practice for some of the girls to live in the Superintendents House to put into practice their training, prior to obtaining a position outside the colony. It was in this environment that Mr and Mrs Higgins found themselves not only pampered by a Housekeeper and servants, but also treated like Lord and Lady of the Manor.

Continuing in the tradition of the Guardians, the M.E.C. in a planned economy, suggested that the Headship of the School be included with the duties of Superintendent of the Homes and accordingly Mr Higgins signature as Headmaster was required in the School Log Book each week. In the absence of Mr Higgins from the school, Mr Smith was permitted to assume the title of Headmaster in name only, as his official title was still Assistant Head. Mr Smith may not have approved of the arrangements and may have even resented this snub by the new ruling body of the Styal Homes. However, so far as the pupils of the school were concerned, he was in command and carrying out the job he had always assumed would be his, So far as can be ascertained Mr Higgins did not encroach on Mr Smith's territory and left the running of the school entirely in his hands. On just one occasion at the beginning of 1934, Mr Higgins intervened with a direct order that the practice of saluting the Headmaster was to be discontinued and that the children were to march into assembly as other schools did. During the first term of office Mr Higgins proudly announced that an astonishing number of 21 pupils had passed scholarships to Manchester schools. A few weeks later, the end of term Draper Cups were awarded to the best all round pupils and Mr Higgins took great delight in presenting two medals to Kenneth Jones and Margaret Alker. The demilitarisation of the children of Styal was uppermost in the mind of the Superintendent but at the same time he was reminded of the rules of the colony in keeping with his £1,000 per year salary. Those rules which in all circumstances were to be adhered to without question were the propagation of a) Drill, b) Discipline, c) Religious Instruction, d) Routine Housework.

Within the confines of the sleepy hamlet of Styal, where topics of conversation borded on the local Cricket Team or the awards made to the prize winning market gardeners, 1935 proved to be a never forgotton year of drama, suspense and intrigue. The first indication of what was to become the centre stage of gossip was the declaration by the M.E.C. that the well respected Chaplain of the Homes, was undergoing a nervous breakdown. After a period of two months, during which time a host of well wishers had made known their sympathies, an almost unbelievable rumour had begun to circulate at the two colonies. The disappearance of a Children's Home Mother and the reported illness of the Padre had produced stories of outrageuos proportion, so much so, that the committee of the Homes were forced into declaring that the Church Minister of Styal Homes had been de-frocked. The scandal which surrounded the elopement of the Home Mother and the Vicar became a sensational headline amongst the adult population, whilst every step was taken to suppress the news from the children. Only one other scandal in the history of Styal had ever attained or superseded the dimensions of the present event. At that time, over sixty years ago, under the reign of Edward Hyde Greg, two local youths who worked at the Quarry Bank Mill, were making their way home after the Sunday evening choir practice. A girl aged 19, the daughter of a local farmer, was also on her way home after the Easter Sunday rehearsal. What happened next became headlines in the newspapers and notoriety for the two local lads. Although the incident - according to the youths - had been a frolic, the papers outlined the Sunday saga as 'an outrageous attempt of assault and rape'. As a result of the publicity and the shame which had been placed on the families and the village, the boys, fully awarc of the police search and the future court trial, made their way to Liverpool. Perhaps the destiny of the Styal pals from Quarry Bank lay in the last comments of the newspaper reports 'It is now rumoured that the two Styal Boys have run away and are now believed to be living in America'.

The Styal Homcs wes host to the second drama of the year when, three days before Armistice Day the former plumber at the Colony was found lying by thc pond in front of the Lodge House. His throat had been cut and there was a pen knife lying next to his body. After an inquiry it was disclosed that Mr Pollit, aged 56, the Homes Plumber since 1915, had committed suicide. As if to end the year on a brighter theme, the Styal Homes Girl Guides (1st Styal Company) on the 29th November and to commemorate the Silver Jubilee of King George Vth and Queen Mary, planted a 'Bird Cherry' tree in the Church gardens. Mr Higgins conducted the service under the direction of Capt Mrs Frazer and Lt Miss Coleman.

It was during a council meeting in Manchester that a major decision was accepted and new proposals were advocated for the future of the Styal Homes. The 1936 committee, which had taken into account the social changes of that period and the fact that only 416 children were in residence at the 630 bed accommodation at Styal, concluded that the new Homes at Styal which had been built for the Swinton Children, should be annexed into a separate establishment. The further suggestion was that a) the physically defective children from the Homes at Mobberley and Heaton Mersey be assembled at Styal and b) the new colony be known as the 'Residential Open Air School' for Delicate Children. Of the two other decisions concerning the Styal Homes one of these was a proposal that the orphan babies of Manchester, now in residence at Dr Rhodes Home should be sent to Styal Institution. The other and final change to the social structure was the transfer of all scholarship children from Styal, who now resided at the Rhodes Home, to be boarded out with foster parents. Another two years were to elapse before the change-over was complete and by 1938, the new inmates of Styal had settled in to their own segregated colony which nested between the Styal Homes and Oakwood Farm. Like the Homes institution, the entrance was adorned with two huge iron gates.

During 1936, a year which was steeped in national and international intrigue concerning the Royal Family and the throne of England, the Homes were to receive their fourth full time Chaplain. He was Mr H. Saxon, formerly of Manchester, and his duties commenced on the 22nd April. Meanwhile, the acting Headmaster, Mr Smith was given leave by the Manchester Education Committee to make a tour of the schools in Manchester in order that he might learn up to date teaching methods which might benefit the isolated children of the Homes. What Mr Smith learned from his two month vacation is not recorded. However, as a result of his findings the House System was adopted by the senior school on the 28th October 1936. This new democracy allowed the children to take part in a voting process which resulted in the election of a School Captain and four Prefects for the boys and the same facility for the girls. At this first ever inauguration, the two Captains were given the platform and their names entered on the School Roll of Honour. They were Bertha Baxter (girls) Sidney Schofield (boys). The four 'Houses' and their associated colour were named as: Nightingale - (Nobility of character) Shakespeare - (Literature) Marconi - (Invention) Scott - (Exploration). Together with the Football Cup and the Draper Cup, another Cup given to the School by the M.E.C. and which was to become symbolic as a 'House' competition. Unfortunately and probably due to this latest innovation, the Draper Silver Medal ceased to be an annual competition for the individual scholar and became just a memory of the old system and the Manchester Guardians. As far as can be ascertained, the very last presentation of the 'Draper' silver medal was to a boy by the name of Kenneth Adderley. The name of the girl is unknown.

From a child's point of view, 1938 was a good year, especially when referring to May 31st. That day, Styal Cottage Homes and representatives of the M.E.C. paid homage and gave a toast to the retiring 'Old Soldier' and Bandmaster of the Institution. According to the officials, he had been the kingpin and the most influential person in the history of the colony. Mr Cochran, according to the committee, was leaving a piece of history at Styal and in addition a world wide family of both military and civilian bandsman who had benefited from his talents. The departure of Mr Cochran to Barlow Road, Lacey Green, Wilmslow, meant far more to the waving children who breathed a sigh of relief. Gone forever was the military 'sergeant major' with the stick of torture and a reputation of physical cruelty. Who was to be his replacement was the question uppermost in the minds of the children. Hardly one week had passed since Mr Cochran had made his exit when his successor, entered the gates of the colony for the first time. Looking every inch a civilian and a quiet spoken young intellectual, Mr C.H. Dawe's arrival was announced. From first impressions it would seem as though the old method of employing an ex Band Master come Drill Inspector had at last given way to a modern and more humane approach. This was to be partially true since Mr Dawe had been offered the position as Band Master so long as he was willing to reside at one of the Home Cottages together with his wife and two young children. This seemingly modern day approach to child welfare was a concept of the old Chorlton Guardians, who in 1896. had decreed that every cottage should be supervised by a Mother and Father couple. Now, forty years on, the process had begun, but like the Guardians, Manchester Education Committee were well aware of the financial impracticality of staffing every home on a similar basis. Mr Dawe did have a military connection but the children, like the staff, were ignorant to the fact that he was a former Band and Orchestra musician of the Royal Rifle Brigade. However, it was his musical talents that brought him to Styal and as a result of his military training he and his family set up home as Father and Mother to the older boys of the Homes.

With the departure of Mr Cochran and the death at Norcliffe Hall in 1934 of Colonel Ernest Greg, one could be justified in claiming this period of Styal's history to be 'the end of an era'. Since the other death of Mr H.P. Greg of Lode Hill in 1936, Alexander Greg, the son of Col. Ernest Greg, transferred the ownership of Quarry Bank Estate to the National Trust.

CHAPTER 13

THE LAST POST

In spite of the tiring work schedules by every boy and girl in the Colony and the relentless punishment by some House Mothers and the sadistic Mr Smith of the Senior School, the young duo of Mr Higgins and Mr Dawe were slowly but surely guiding the outdated institution of Styal Homes towards a more progressive future and liberal attitude to child welfare. This promise of a brighter for the children of the system was brought to a sudden ending when, during August of 1939, the holiday at Squires Gate was cut short by the proclamation of the second world war. From that moment on, the Styal Homes Colony was unavoidably caught up in the crisis of the nation. The ticking clock of progress was silenced and in its wake the colony slipped into a decline which was to last a decade. Behind this curtain of isolation, the occupants of the Houses became once again, prisoners of circumstances. Every spadeful of earth removed for the purpose of trench building, symbolised a step backwards in the foundation of what appeared to be an outpost settlement on the Cheshire Plains. Since Styal Homes was an establishment with a long pedigree of isolation, the War did not have the impact which was felt by the civilisation outside the gates of the colony. Nevertheless, changes did occur at the Homes, many of them still vividly remembered by the former children of that period. Amongst some of those changes which at that time seemed insignificant were such things as; the removal of the enormous iron gates at the entrance which, as was discovered years later, were claimed by the War Office for ammunition making. Almost overnight an array of concrete air raid shelters sprang up throughout the colony and an Air Raid Siren of huge dimensions was mounted on the roof of the Homes Boiler House. The siren not only gave a warning to the Homes, but also to Styal Village and the surrounding neighbours of Handforth and Wilmslow. City evacuees swelled the number of inmates to an all time capacity of over six hundred, but the average of 530 children remained during the war.

1940 and 1941 proved to be the most crucial years in Manchester during the onslaught of the enemy bombing blitz and these were the most telling years at Styal Homes. Many were the nights which were seemingly cold and endless, when teeth chattered and overcoats were buttoned tightly to keep the frightened children warm.

Big Mr Higgins, - 'The Boss' as he was now referred to by the inmates - dressed in his A.R.P. uniform and tin helmet brought a reassuring feeling of security as he made his nightly round to every cottage or 'dug-out' shelter. The steady droning of the enemy bombers became synonymous with every air raid warning, yet, somehow the early morning 'all clear' siren, signalled the dawning of a new day, and nature's dawn chorus leavened the fears and anxieties of the night.

What can now be seen to be one of Styal's unique moments of history, took place on Wednesday April the 8th, 1941. Just moments away from teatime, the children and workers at the Homes hastily scrambled to the shelters by the wailing of air raid siren. During the half an hour or so whilst waiting for the all clear, a loud noise was heard at close range and the concrete bunkers vibrated to the impact of Styal's first and only bombing of the war. Down at the village at about the time of impact, two local inhabitants were stood chatting near to the Ship Inn. In the course of their duties as village Policeman and village Home Guard, P.C. Sam Pickering and Mr Jim Mottram, who ran the local shoe shop next to the Post Office, were well aware of the German aircraft which had just passed over the village but were uncertain about the cause of the explosion. Later that evening, Jim Mottram was to learn that not only had a bomb dropped on Styal by the stray aircraft but another bomb had fallen on a house at Water Lane, Wilmslow. The bomb in Wilmslow failed to explode and the whole area was evacuated by the military authorities whilst it was defused. Another day passed before Mr Mottram learned that the house in Wilmslow had been occupied by a relation of his mother, his mother being a direct descendant of the old Styal family of Venables. The first children to learn of the near miss of the enemy bomber were the boys of the senior class of the school. Having been excused lessons for the morning, they were marched from the school complete with spades and shovels, back in the direction of the Homes and down the steep slope of Twinneys Brow. Mr Jones, the Sports Master, ordered the boys to climb over the sty just prior to the bridge over the river Dean. Once in the field of Norcliffe Farm, the view of the giant crater caused both excitement and consternation. Had the bomb fallen two or three hundred yards eastwards, it would have scored a direct hit on the Cottage Homes. About fifty yards westward, the target would have been the entrace to the Quarry Bank Woods of the National Trust.

Manchester's well established bus service to Styal came to a halt during 1941. It was to be another eight years before the No. 64 bus resumed its service to the village cenotaph. The cessation of the bus service contributed still further to the isolation of Styal and from that moment on, staffing at the Styal Homes and the Schools was to become a major problem. Even the Saturday visiting by relatives of the children was curtailed, due to the long one and a half mile walk from Moss Nook terminal. A most unusual event took place on the 29th April 1941, when the whole of the senior school were summoned to the main hall of the school in order that they might listen to a radio broadcast performed by the military Band of the Manchester Regiment. This live broadcast, it had been explained, was of particular interest to the Styal Homes because of the number of old boys now serving with the Manchester's. Four weeks before the end of the summer term, the news arrived from the M.E.C. that two girls, Vera Hadfield and Sylvia Brown had won a place at the Central High School in Manchester and nine other children had been nominated for places at Ducie Avenue School. For the older boys of the senior school, 1941 saw the start of a new subject entered into the curriculum during the months of September and October. Its title was: 'Potato Picking' This employment of children on the Homes Farm resulted from the national labour shortage and the campaign to grow more food. However, the boys did receive payment for their backbreaking services and the going rate for the following eight years was one penny per hour.

On the retirement of Mr Saxon in 1942, manchester Corporation asked the young minister of St Chad's Church at Handforth, if he would assume the duties of part time Chaplain to the Styal Cottage Homes, to which he agreed. Mr Roger Frith's part time chaplaincy was somehow able to accommodate the three church services every Sunday, and the religious teaching at the school. He was a popular figure amongst the children as was the ageing Mr Taylor, the organist cum Choir Master since 1898. The Ship Adoption Society scheme was established during 1939 when schools throughout the country were given the opportunity to adopt a Merchant Ship for mutual interest and exchange letters and gifts. At that time, Styal School was given it's first contact with the outside world and rewarded with their own ship. In June of 1943, Mr Stevenson of the Ship Adoption Society paid a visit to the School in the company of a respresentative of the Anglo Saxon Petroleum Company. His mission on that day, was to present to the Styal Homes, a framed photograph of their adopted ship M.V. 'Miralda' and also to thank the children of the school for their sacks of letters and comforts (gifts) for the sailors and crew. Two years later on Friday 13th July 1945, Mr Stevenson made his second visit to the Styal Homes School to make a special presentation. For the first time in the history of the school, a photographer from the Advertiser recorded this unique moment. In the words of Mr Stevenson 'he knew of no other school whose connection with the Ship Adoption Society had been more helpful and consistent than theirs had been. Today's event was the award of a Ship's Shield from the crewmen of the Miralda. The Shield, which had been specially made by the crew, displayed a large shell as its centrepeice and an airman's wings underneath, flanked on either side by blue coloured Swordfish. The Swordfish were to typify the aircraft carried by the vessel which operated against the enemy submarine fleets'. The recipients of the Ship's Shield were the two School Captains, Doreen Barber and Kenneth Webb.

Unlike the First World War, the boys of the Homes escaped the militarism associated with that era and only the Band boys were being recruited for service. Nevertheless an attempt was made by a member of the M.E.C. to compel the boys of 14 years of age to establish an Army Cadet Company in the Styal village. The minutes of that committee meeting revealed the verdict as 'there are too few boys over the age of fourteen and it is not desirable for children of the colony associating with an outside organisation'. The grey coloured barrage balloons dotted the skyline around Styal for much of the war and it was not unusual to see hordes of Parachutists making their practice descents. Also, the landscape around Styal was host to the now familiar blue uniformed men and women of the Air Force. Sometime during the 1943 period, the American soldiers made their appearance in and around Wilmslow and Alderley districts of Cheshire, and for a short time, even camped on the Styal Homes estate. For as long as the ex Homes children of the war period survive, they will undoubtedly cherish the memory of the American soldiers who befriended them. It all began with an accidental meeting of the Homes Chaplain Roger Frith and the American Padre Clifford Frith of Maryland in the U.S.A. Padre Frith was the senior chaplain to the American forces who were scattered around Wilmslow districts and it was the probable coincidence of their names which brought about their first introduction. After an invitation by Mr Frith of St Chad's to the U.S. Padre, a group of American soldiers attended a service at the Handforth church. It became just a matter of time before the same group of American soldiers and the Padre made an entrance at the Styal Cottage Homes. From that moment on, the children of the colony forged a friendship with the soldiers and for the first time in the history of the institution, an outside charitable organisation had pentrated the system. To the children, not used to any form of luxury excepting the one penny spends every Saturday, the chocolate, the chewing gum, the sweets and the coins of three pences and sixpences, became manna from heaven, from the ever generous G.I.'s. At the Christmas concert, the Americans contributred to the Christmas Tree presents which were provided by the Manchester Corporation and Child Welfare charities. Towards the end of the evening Mr Dawe led the Band into the rendering of the American National Anthem and the Canadian National Anthem. The bond of friendship grew stronger with every visit by the soldiers, both at the weekly cinema show and the church services. The affair came to a sudden ending, almost as spontaneous as its beginnings. Days and dates are now forgotton, but somewhere in the memories of yesteryear, Styal's warm flourishing Springtime whispered a final farewell.

Maytime of 1944 signalled the mass exodus of military personnel from all over the country and it was this migration to the south of England which included the Padre Frith and the G.I.'s of Wilmslow. In the absence of newspapers or wireless sets and the restricted communications with the outside world, the children were ignorant of world affairs and the war in general. Almost two months went by before the Homes Chaplain gave the news to the children that he had received a letter from Padre Clifford Frith of the American Forces. In a subdued manner and with a quiet voice, Mr Frith interpreted the contents of the letter at the Sunday service. The news could not have been worse. Explaining the 'D'- Day invasion of the 6th June, Padre Frith was sorry to have to break the news that from all the American soldiers who had been associated with the Styal Homes, he alone, was the sole survivor, and all the soldiers had been killed at the landings at Cherbourg. At a leter date, it was disclosed that the American Chaplain had received the Purple Heart for his part during the invasion. In retrospect, maybe the American soldiers had not died in vain, as their efforts to win the affections of the children had not gone unnoticed. The M.E.C. encouraged the future liaison between the Homes boys and girls, and the local units of the W.A.A.F. and R.A.F. who readily accepted the challenge to continue from where the G.I.'s had left off. Almost twelve months to the day of the 'D' Day invasion, Capt. Bloom and Corporal Patton of the U.S. Army made a special visit to the Colony and made a presentation of a collection of photographs which had been left behind by the fallen heroes. True to form, the V.E. celebrations signalling the end of the War were predictably carried out at both the Styal colonies, and the Armistice Day service at the Homes in 1945 was of special significance to the children. Names of boys, some of them familiar, who had fallen during the second world war were mentioned by Mr Frith and Mr Higgins, with a promise that at a later date they would be added to the Roll of Honour. Reference was also made to the boys who had been decorated for gallantry and it was not surprising that Mr Higgins brought up the name of Michael Wood a former Band Boy of Mr Cochran's era. He had joined the Kings Own Royal Regt. in 1936. His achievement whilst serving as a Captain in the West Yorkshire Regiment had resulted in the award of the coveted Military Cross.

The Curtis Report which was published in September 1946 was an interim report into the Care of Children throughout England and Wales. Under the chairmanship of Myra Curtis, C.B.E., the seventeen committee members, including Miss Kingsmill Jones O.B.E., an Alderman and former Lord Mayor of Manchester, presented their findings and recommendations to the Government Ministers of the day, being: Secretary of State for the Home Department, Rt. Hon J. Chuter Ede, M.P., Minister of Health, the Rt Hon. Aneurin Bevan M.P., Minister of Education, the Rt Hon Ellen Wilkinson, M.P. The foundations of the Curtis Report dated back to the 8th March 1945 when, under the recommendation of Herbert morrison M.P., the committee was set up to inquire into existing methods of providing for children who from loss of parents or from any cause whatever are deprived of a normal home life with their own parents or relatives; and to consider what further measures should be taken to ensure that these children are brought up under conditions best calculated to compensate them for the lack of parental care. As a result of the Government acceptance of the Curtis Report, the central control of normally healthy children (with certain exceptions) was transferred to one Government Department, namely, the Home Office. After the implementation of several parliamentary bills derived from the Curtis Report, the long awaited 'Children Act' became law on 5th July 1948.

The effects of the Curtis Report in connection with the Styal Cottage Homes, were to say the least, devastating. Conclusive proof had been obtained by the 1945/6 committee to warrant an immediate investigation into the future of the Homes colony. Time and facts have since revealed that 1946 and the Curtis Report were responsible for the beginning of the end of the Styal Homes and its final agonising decade. Other contributory factors made 1946 the most crucial year in the entire history of the Homes. Cracks were about to become crevices, molehills set to become mountains, streams of frustration were destined to become rivers of human conflict, and all leading to the inevitable downfall of Manchester's last isolated child colony of Victorian Institutionalism. Even the normally placid rivers of the Dean and Bollin became raging torrents of flood devastation, causing chaos in the valleys around the Homes perimeter. It was this setting which coincided with an ultimatum from the Superintendent addressed to the committee of the Manchester Education Department. As a result of his strongly worded communication he was summonsed to the Town Hall to explain the dilemma at the Styal Homes. At the special hearing, he refused point blank to allow any more children to be permitted to enter the gates of Styal until extra Housemothers and Staff was found. Such was the crisis, he explained, that most of the present staff at the Homes had not had their annual leave and most of them were working over sixty hours per week. The committee responded with a promise to advertise for additional labour but at the same time they were aware of the inaccessibility of Styal's isolated colony and the competition for better paid jobs in the town and cities. In the meantime, Mr Higgins was advised to make full use of the workforce of the children, especially those aged fourteen and over.

Continuing the concluding evidence of the Curtis Rpeort, the observations with regard to Styal was as follows - 'The Cottage Homes' considered to be the answer to the old Barrack system of the last century, were built to house children from the age of two years to 15 years. It was noticable however that there was a tendency to increase the size of units in this kind of home. For many reasons such as the difficulty of boarding out or shortage of staff, the cottage units were larger than was regarded as desirable. They were rapidly losing the character of small households and becoming small institutions while at the same time the buildings were very overcrowded. A group of thirty children aged between two and fourteen years, becomes a very different problem of management compared to the planned group home of fifteen children'

'The Cottage Homes were unhomely in appearance and set out in grounds which were formal and forbidding, with large main gates of institutional type, asphalt driveways and a lack of opportunity from variety and privacy. We were told by the urban Grouped Cottage Home that visits by the Home children to outside local children were discouraged because the Homes children picked up bad manners. The visitor was told that the spending money of between one penny and threepence had so little value that the older boys and girls who were allowed a Saturday afternoon in neighbouring Wilmslow found that there were great limitations to purchases. The general view, that it is a serious handicap to children to be too much isolated from the community to which they will eventually return, seems to have been accepted by the staffs of the Homes. Finally, it was accepted that in all the institutions for children including Styal, the most frequent and persistent complaint was enuresis (bed wetting) and the forms of punishment varied in each establishment'.

1946 became a litter bed of frustrations and problems for the Superintendent of the Homes, the main culprits being staff shortages, a non-existent bus service, and the increase in the numbers of boys and girls who were running away from the Homes. A major disaster of another kind almost took place during the Autumn when the Styal landscape was shattered by an airplane crash. On 4th of October an aircraft which had just taken off on a routine flight to Belfast, suddenly lost height as it passed over Styal village. Without any warning, it avoided the rooftops of Shaws Fold, collided with the treetops on either side of Styal Road, and finally ploughed into the Homes potato harvest, missing the school building by approximately 100 yards.; Many of the senior school children witnessed the crash and two of the teachers, Mr Jardine and Mr Duffy, raced accross the playground to rescue the pilot. In retrospect, the most ironic aspect of the incident was the absence of any children who, for the past four years had always been employed as potato pickers, during the first few weeks of October. Had they been in the fields that day there would have been a major disaster. On the credit side of the year and in full knowledge of the Curtis Committee's investigation the 'Boss' set about the task of easing the tensions and making life for both the children and the Housemothers more bearable. Several events took place during the year which included the requisition of ambulances for the sick mothers who were in Crumpsall and Withington Hospitals, to be transported to visit their children at Styal; All the children over the age of eight years were given a day's outing on the 17th July in order that they could walk the two miles to where the King and Queen were passing the neighbourhood. A request was made to the committee for the resumption of holidays to the seaside; it was deferred until the following year; another request to the committee by the Boss was for the installation of new solid fuel cookers to be in every cottage at Styal Homes, to replace the outdated Swinton Black Ranges; The Homes Choir boys and girls were allowed to have an annual days outing which consisted of a trip to Prestbury and then a hike to Alderley Edge Copper Mines, finishing with tea at the Wizard Tea Rooms before walking back to Styal. The Bonfire celebrations of November the 5th which had always been the highlight of the Homes calendar were re-introduced. The progress of the year was even more accentuated by the success of the Junior Football Team over Manchester Grammar School and the victorious Cricket Team who were also the winners of a Manchester Grammar meeting. According to the minutes of the 1946 log book, 'the first issue of bananas was made at the Styal Cottage Homes and all the children appeared to like them'. After a year of constant reference by the media to the Curtis Investigation on Child Care, the first real breakthrough came to Styal just prior to the New Year. Mr Higgins and the M.E.C. had embarked upon an innovation which would bring together the isolated children of Styal and the General Public of Manchester. This scheme which carried the grand title 'Surrogate Aunties and Uncles for the Styal Children', began its operations at the Christmas period when no fewer than 60 boys and girls were selected to spend the festive season with their foster guardians.

Lindow Common, the site of one of the great archaeological finds of the 20th Century became a Winter Wonderland during 1947. Nature had produced one of the coldest winters ever recorded and in so doing, had transformed the small lake into a skaters paradise. The all familiar yellow broom and gorse scrubland of the Summer now lay petrified under the overcoat of the heavy Winter Frost. Needless to say, the Homes children availed themselves of Lindow's offerings and also partook of the sledging conditions of Carrs Wood. After a long harsh winter and a measles epidemic, the children of the Colony were completely taken by surprise with an announcement by the Superintendent. The boys and girls could not believe their ears when they were informed that the Saturday Penny was to cease at the end of March and a completely new rate of pocket money was to be introduced. The scale, in connection with the children of Styal was to be thus;-

under seven years of age	-	one penny per week
seven to twelve years	-	threepence per week
thirteen years	-	sixpence per week
fourteen years	-	one shilling per week
fifteen years	-	two shillings and sixpence per week.

Much to the disappointment of Mr Higgins the holidays to the seaside did not materialise but compensations were made in other pursuits., For one thing, M.E.C. allowed Styal School to be included amongst the Manchester Schools Annual Sports Day at Belle Vue and still further encouraged the pupils of the Senior School to enter competitions in the local districts of Alderley and Wilmslow. Within the first two years of the inter school liaison three girls became outstanding in the history of the Homes. Jeanette Watson not only won a handwriting competition in a national Children's Newspaper but also scored a success in the 100 yards race at Belle Vue. The other two girls who won first and second place in an open air 'painting' competition at Wilmslow and Alderley Flower Show were Venia Myers and Marjorie Ralphson.

Offerings of outings, treats and presents fell upon the Styal children like confetti at the Christmastime of 47, not least of which was an invitation from the B.B.C. in Piccadilly, Manchester. Forty boys and girls together with the Superintendent and Matron, were guests at the B.B.C. Christmas Day Party Broadcast and the entertainers for the afternoon included: Mr Gerald Iles,, curator of Belle Vue Zoo, Mr Jack Watson, B.B.C. broadcaster, Mr Albert Modley, Comedian, and Miss Violet (Auntie Violet) Carson pianist. Other outings included a circus show at Belle Vue, the children being the guests of the Manchester Evening Chronicle. Two pantomime treats provided by the Manchester Committee took place at the Ardwick Hippodrome and the Rex Cinema at Wilmslow, and in the old tradition, there was separate showings for boys and girls. One special occasion was the film show at the Odeon on January 3rd 1948, when the proprietors invited 250 children to the preview of Walt Disney's Fun and Fancy Free. For one little girl of the Homes who during the evening, presented a bouquet to the Lord Mayor of Manchester, a mystery evolved which was to cause great consternation to the Police and the Superintendant and Matron of Styal Homes. At the end of the evening's performance, the little girl was missing, only to be found on Bury Electric Railway Station a few hours later. No explanation was ever given for the reasons behind the dissappearance and it was the next day before she was escorted back to Styal.

Manchester Education Committee relinquished its parentage of the Styal Cottage Homes on July 5th 1948. The newly formed Children's Committee took over the administration of the colony and the children became the wards of their new Guardians for the fifth and final time. In readiness for the takeover, the Children's Committee of Manchester Town Hall had already begun their operations with the formation of the Committee on the 23rd March, when they elected Mr I.H.D. Brown as Children's Officer. All the reforms and restructure of the Child Welfare System signalled a new phase in child establishments, and Styal was about to receive its first injection of 20th Century involvement. Over the next few years, the Homes were inundated with trainee students specialising in child welfare, Probation Officers, House Mothers, and Social Science pupils. At last the seaside holiday was included in the 1948 itinerary, the boys and girls each enjoying their separate two week stay at the Abergele Holiday Camp. The year's agenda also included a Bertram Mills Circus visit to Platt Fields for 200 girls and a tour of Ringway Airport, for the boys. Breaking the long tradition of the Homes, the last boys to enlist in Army Bands were interviewed by Captain Spooner of the 2nd Bn Manchester Regiment, and for the very last time Mr Dawe escorted the two lads to Ladysmith Barracks, Ashton under Lyne.

Styal's village policeman since 1944 was P.C. Waite, who had exchanged his area of Henbury near Macclesfield, with P.C. Sam Pickering of Styal. He and his wife and family occupied the Police House near the Post Office where he had settled down to being a familiar figure in and around the village. His presence was also known to the boys and girls of the Homes, especially around the time when the fruit trees were in full harvest and on the occasions when children absconded from the Colony. To the children, his bark was louder and worse than his bite, for in all his nine years at Styal, before his transfer to Lymm in 1953 there was never any reason to think of him as being anything other than the friendly village copper.

Unknown to the children P.C. Waite patrolled the ground of Styal Homes every night during May of 1948. The reason behind this unusual activity came about after a little girl had been murdered in the grounds of a Blackburn hospital and the order had been issued by the Children's Committee to lock all doors and windows at night and to request the assistance of the local policemen for security during the hours of darkness.

Reformation was beginning to take root at the Styal Homes in a way which seemed unhurried. Yet, as the 20th century curtains opened wider, the creeping vines of change were already developing their stranglehold around the beleaguered colony. So far, the children had benefited from the new ideas of the Children's Committee and there was still further hint of emancipation from the shackles of the Homes outdated institutionalism.

Unfortunately, the price of change has never been cheap, and whilst the credit side looked healthy for the children, the effects upon the staff at Styal were disasterous. Records for the year of 1948, show an exodus of twenty four adults who either resigned or retired as a direct result of the proposed new legislation for the future running of the establishment. Many of the older employees, who were associated with the old Manchester Guardians, joined in the migration as did Mr Park of the Oakwood Farm who left with his family to live in Preston. Almost ten years to the day, Mr Dawe, the Band Master and Drill Instructor, made his exit from the Homes, causing further chaos and concern to Superintendent and Matron Higgins. Whilst the boss made his repeated demands for an increase in staff the general mood throughout the Homes again reached epidemic proportions of deterioration. In response, the Committee acknowledged the deficiency in staff to meet all the requirements of so many children and pointed out that until the full complement of staff was acquired it would be impossible to execute all the changes contributing to the proper care and maintenance of the children at Styal. Knowing of the plight of the workforce at Styal, the Children's Committee made some efforts to improve conditions by way of the following recommendations: "In connection with the shortage of staff at Styal Cottage Homes, the Children's Committee agreed to provide additional recreational activities and a motor vehicle which could be used to transport staff between the Cottage Homes and the bus stop. Apart from a limited service to the station at Styal, the terminus for the bus service connecting Styal with Manchester is approximately 1½ miles from the Homes. On winter nights the staff were reluctant to spend their off duty time in Manchester owing to the transport difficulties. It is hoped that the provision of the vehicle will assist the staff in this matter". Still continuing on the Styal Homes staff crisis, the Committee issued another statement which seemed to sum up their feelings of frustration: "Employees who have received their initial training at Styal and upon whom a lot of time and patience has been spent by older members of the staff, have left to take posts with local authorities where their duties are so much lighter, because of the smaller number of children in their charge. Often these other Homes are situated in places which offer greater facilities for their leisure time by virtue of the proximity to shops, communications and places of amusement.'

With the departure of Mr Dawe, the once famous Styal Homes Military Band slipped quietly into a state of decline, and even the attempts of Mr Fell the part time Bandmaster, failed to revive the majestic echoes of its musical past. During the Armistice day service at the Church, the leading cornet player gave his usual rendering of the Last Post and Reveille. Two weeks later, towards the end of November 1949, the Bugler, Jimmy Brown, walked the well trodden path to the central point of the Homes, and for the very last time in the history of the Colony, sounded the 7pm 'Last Post' indicating Bedtime and Lights Out. In May of 1955, Manchester Education Committee purchased the whole of the Band instruments for £300, and subsequently placed them with the Greenheys school. A further rise in the scale of pocket money made 1949 another memorable year with the new allowances being substituted:-

Up to 5 years	-	3d per week and 4oz of sweets
5 to 7 years	-	6d per week and 4oz of sweets
8 to 12 years	-	1s 3d per week
13 years	-	1s 9d per week
14 years	-	2s 3d per week
15 years	-	3s 0d per week

Other schemes which had received the approval of the Children's Committee included the installation of the wireless set in each of the cottages at Styal, for the exclusive use of the children. By the generosity of the Lord Mayor's Fund, every girl in the Homes took great delight in the Christmas present of a dressed doll, the first time in their lives they had ever possessed a luxury. The Commitee approved yet another idea for the benefit of the children in care and in 1950, inaugerated the first ever issue of a birthday card and present to be sent by post to every child. Included in the wholesale action of the Children's Committee to improve and provide better conditions for the children of Styal Homes, a new ruling was adopted regarding the maintenance of discipline. From the 1st December 1949, and for the first time in Manchester, discipline in Homes provided by the authority was to be maintained without resort to corporal punishment. This remarkable piece of legislation should have been the climax to the Christmas of 1949 but evidence points to a three year delay in the application of this ruling at Styal Homes.

On hearing the news of the suggested reorganisation at the Styal Homes during 1951, another spate of resignations was handed to the Committee, the most notable ones being the Homes Hospital nursing staff. Mr Frith of St Chads, Handforth, received his transfer notice and on the 8th June ceased his ministerial duties at the Homes Church. The new look theme for a continuing futuristic outlook at the Styal Colony, was approved by Mr Brown the Children's Officer, on the 20th April. Extracts from the ten page supplement are as follows:-

a "It is the intention of the Committee to reduce the size of Styal Cottage Homes so as to enable the children to develop their own individuality.

b The Committee is well aware of the dissadvantages of large isolated grouped cottage homes like Styal, situated in a community. It is necessary at the earliest stage to form mixed homes instead of the separated boys from girls regime.

c A new scale for the proposed number of children in each of the 22 cottages, ie, homes with 30 children to be halved, those numbering 24, to be reduced to 16 children and the homes which contain 14 children, to be reduced to ten in total.

d Introduce married couples only

e Every child to have a cooked breakfast every day of the week.

f All House mothers to receive a course of cookery lessons.

g No tasks to be carried out by the children until after breakfast, including bed making.

h No washing up by children after dinner and breakfast on school days, and the lavatory cleaning to be assigned to staff cleaners.

i Older children from the age of thirteen to forego supervision at bath time and to have complete privacy.

j The censorship of children's letters in and out of the Homes to be discontinued.

An approximate figure of £45,000 was allocated by the General Purposes Committee to the Homes Estate for improvements and modernisation and Norcliffe Farm received its first supply of electricity and two new shippons. Benefits for the staff and children varied from house to house but generally, all the outdated cooking stoves were replaced by new Glow Warm Cookers, bedside lockers were provided for all children in which to store their belongings and a host of other changes included curtains, wardrobes, bedside rugs and an up to date recreation room. To the delight of the children new rules allowed for the keeping of pets and such was the importance of the scheme , a news reporter was allowed into the colony to photograph the children with their pet rabbits. Without doubt the crowning glory of 1951 was the advent of the bicycle. The Children's Committee had known for some time that adolescent children of 15 and 16 years of age were leaving the Styal Institution, totally unable to ride a bicycle. This inexperience of bicycles was put forward at an inquest of a Styal boy who, at the age of 15, wobbled off his new bicycle and was run over by a lorry, receiving fatal injuries. Never in the history of the Homes had such records been set for absconding. Minutes for 1950 and 1951 showed as many as 25 cases per month of running away, although the weekly average remained at a constant two or three. Most boys or girls were returned by the Manchester Police the next day but in some cases P.C. Waite apprehended the would-be absconders and escorted them to the security of the institution.

1951 had been a very notable year in terms of past 'old boys' and 'old girls' who in some cases, had travelled thousands of miles to visit the place of their childhood upbringing. One ex Home boy, a former inmate of Myrtle Cottage, had come from Australia, where he was employed as a Harbour Pilot. Others included Merchant Navy Officers, Army Bandmasters and some residents of New Zealand, South Africa and Canada. A woman by the name of Leila Taylor, employed as a Sister of a New York hospital, revealed that she had been sent to Canada in 1906 after a memorable childhood at Styal and could remember the visit of Mrs Pankhurst to the Homes. By co-incidence the Christmas party at the Homes brought about the reunion of three former boys who appeared to have been successful in their careers. Harold Varley, a prominent member of the Burnage Rugby Club and a future serving member of Wilmslow District Council, met up at the Homes with his boyhood pal Harry Swann. 'Sunny' Swann, a Band Leader, had brought his ten piece orchestra from the Ritz Ballroom in Manchester, to give a concert for the children of the Homes. On the vary same day, another musician turned up in the shape of ex Corporal Frank Sutton of the Manchester Regiment and now a Bandmaster at Kneller Hall School of Music. Each of the former home lads gave a rendering on a variety of instruments and then paid a sentimental visit to their old haunts. Harold Varley returned to Styal two years later to initiate an annual Christmas treat for the Homes boys and girls which was held at the Burnage Rugby Football Club.

Styal Railway Station was renowned for its well kept garden on the platform embankments. The station master and his two assistants donated their spare time towards the annual display of flower arrangement and had won two first prizes in the competition for the best railway station in the North West area. Another four awards for 2nd and 3rd place were won in consecutive years between 1949 and 1952. P.C. Tom Waite father of David, Dianne and Terrence made history in the village by becoming the first ever person to appear on television in a live broadcast, during the early days of the new era. His hobby of making Doll's Houses had earned him a place at the British Craftmanship Exhibition during 1951 and this event was followed up by a talk on the radio, in which he gave a full description of his hobby. During 1953, P.C. Waite, received an invitation by a Leading store in the West end of London, to display his latest handmade Dolls House.

EPILOGUE

From 1952 onwards, the winds of change had already begun to mingle with the breezes which swept the Styal Landscape and like a storm on the horizon, one could sense that the closing chapter of the Styal Cottage Homes would be anything but peaceful. On one hand, a new breed of children were coming to the Styal Homes, bringing with them the knowledge of a society which allowed more freedom and more say in the future world of a new and young generation; in short, the era of the Rock and Roll years had just begun. The Housemothers of the old school were clinging desperately to the foundations of the Institution in an effort to stem the insecurity which accompanied the surging tide of the 20th Century.

Styal Cottage Homes, the reason for its closure and the verdict all belong to a chapter in the annals of the Manchester Children's Welfare Department. Perhaps one day, their story of Styal will be told, and answers to hundreds of questions from former inmates may be provided. For now, a summary of events which occured both at the village colony and the Homes colony between the years 1952 - 1956 provides a true account of the agonising five final years:

1952 - "At the time of the Annual Report there were 343 children in the Homes, the lowest figure since 1904. The Children's Committee reported: "Although Styal Cottage Homes can never be like a normal home because of its plan and situation, the disadvantages are minimised by the compensation of clean country air and excercise. Two more cottages were converted into mixed abodes and the experiment proved to be successful. However, the conduct of the children is not so good, habitual absconders creating a bad influence on other children. The type of children now being sent to Styal are those unsuitable for foster homes and who have a bad standard of conduct'.

July: - The death was reported of Styal's 'Brave Captain' Lt Col R Alex Greg, who passed away at his Hertfordshire Nursing Home.

Sept 13th 1952 - Edwin John Higgins - 'the Boss' - died suddenly at the Homes. His funeral at Styal Homes Church was attended by almost 400 mourners.

Nov 17th 1952 - Styal Homes Senior School will in future be known as 'Bollin County Primary School' and will be administered by the Manchester Education Committee. A spokesman for the Manchester City Council told the Wilmslow Advertiser that the Styal village children would be at liberty to attend the school if they wanted to, although it is expected that only children from the Homes would attend. The 'Oak School' of the village which is officially known as Styal County Primary School and comes under the jurisdiction of Cheshire County Council, made its identity known due to the spate of letters going astray amongst the two Styal schools.

Dec 1952 - The Students Union of Manchester University entertained 180 children of the Homes and after a day in Manchester presented each child with a present of two half pennies. Wilmslow R.A.F. H.Q. put on a pantomime show for 300 children. Manchester Corporation gave a Christmas treat to 130 children by way of a Pantomime show, followed by tea at the Town Hall and Carol singing in the Albert Square.

1953

Jan 9th 1953 - A conference with the Home Office resulted in the following resolution by the Children's Committee: Styal Cottage Homes and Rose Hill Nursery are to be wound down and a plan put into operation for the provision of smaller family units.

Jan 9th - After an application to build more houses at Styal was turned down by the National Trust Council S.B. Jacks, J.P. in a lengthy statement said: "Styal's village atmosphere is being destroyed by the National Trust. The Greg family made Styal and jealously guarded its inhabitants as a community." On another subject, he commented: "The greatest fight had been against the opening of Ringway as an Airport, all in the hope that Styal would be forever preserved in its isolation."

Feb 13th - Daisy Ruth Higgins (Matron) widow of the late Superintendent is retiring after 19 years at the Homes and is going to live at Pipers Ash near Chester.

Feb 13th - Due to the new Government rulings on consumption of Home produced dairy products and the lack of interest by the boys of the Homes to enter into a farming career, a decision was made to sell the Styal Homes Farm Stock. 66 cattle, 74 pigs, 400 hens and all the farm implements were auctioned to buyers as far as Shropshire and North Wales. The Derbyshire Farmers were unable to attend because of heavy snowfall.

March 16th - With one year remaining before retirement Mr Frederick Victor Smith (Smiggy) at the age of 64 and after 42 years service was made Head Teacher, following the death of Mr Higgins.

March - The age old question of Sanitation and out-dated sewage disposal in connection with the cottages of Styal village was highlighted during a recent survey by the Manchester and Stockport Water Authorities.

April 15th - Mr and Mrs Barley began duties today as Superintendent and Matron of the Styal Cottage Homes. The part time Homes Chaplain is Mr B Rees of St Chads, Handforth.

June 12th - The village was informed by the Wilmslow Advertiser of the immenent departure of P.C. Waite. 'Styal people will miss Constable Waite who after nine years as the local bobby has been transferred to Lymm. A familiar figure in the district, Const. Waite has served for 19 years in the Cheshire Constabulary. Aged 42 years and born at Kidsgrove Staffs, he is married and had two boys and a girl. Before coming to Styal, he was stationed at Henbury and Bollington. He will be succeeded by Constable K.G. Gordon of Macclesfield'.

July 1st - Superintendent Mr Barley reported that there had been no cases of absconding for 15 weeks and believed this to be a record in the Homes history.

July 12th - Because of the knowledge of the closure of Styal Cottage Homes, the younger staff are leaving. The position at the Homes is chaotic and the staffing problem is acute.

August 24th - Mr F.V. Smith, headmaster, placed on record his last entry in the school log book. His retirement came after 42 years at the Styal Homes Senior School.

September 1st - Great unrest among the single Home Mothers since only married couples are being accepted as House parents.

November - Attitude of staff remains unsettled and not conducive to the well being of the children. Trouble at the Homes and the problems of staffing are all due to the impending closure of Styal Homes.

December - P.C. (Flash) Gordon of the village, dressed as Father Christmas and delivered sacks of presents to each of the Childrens Homes.

1954

March - Staffing deteriorating. Unless more staff can be found the situation will become impossible.

June - Part time Band master Mr H. Fell gave one month's notice. He said that the children have no interest in the Band and that progress was very poor.

November - There are 239 children residing at the Styal Homes. The Children's Committee has decided to close down the Homes within the next two years and to promote the grouped Family Home system.

November 30th - Mr Brown, the Children's Officer gave a report on the progress of the new Family Group Homes:

'The work of the erection of the first of the family group homes was commenced during the year. Of the 51 homes planned, 45 will be of the 4 bedroom type accomodating 6 children and house parents. All homes will be erected on Manchester Corporation housing estates. The first family group home was opened on the Langley Estate, Middleton in November 1954. It is expected that four homes will be in operation by March 1955 with a further 26 homes under construction. This Annual Report may come to be regarded as 'the end of the beginning'. This 6th report records the opening of a new phase - family group homes, and the breaking up of large residential groups'.

December - It was decided by the Children's Committee that the Church at Styal Homes should lose its anonymity and be known at St Andrews Church Styal.

December - The 'Sunday Pictorial' launched a Christmas gift appeal for those who live in Children's homes. The response was overwhelming, with gifts and visitors pouring in from all of the North West.

1955

There has been a marked improvement in the general conduct of the Styal children, due to a much wider choice of activities and greater leisure pursuits, a better esprit de corps now prevails. The work force at the Homes has to be placated because of acute staffing and even the younger married couples, knowing of the future policy, are leaving or resigning. The work has ceased to be a pleasure. The introduction of the new N.J.C. salary scales which came into being on 1st September 1953 was a landmark in the history of child welfare workers, with improved payment and conditions. However, even this has failed to attract the number of women required to take up

Residential work at Styal.

April 9th 1955 - The death was announced of Mr J Cochran, former Bandmaster of the famouse Styal Homes Military Band. He was 81 years of age.

May 31st - Only 126 children left at the Homes.

June 3rd - Mr Frederick Victor Smith, former Styal Homes Headmaster, died suddenly today. Seven adults from the staff attended his funeral on 6th June.

July 29th - Styal Homes Hospital transferred to the Lodge Home to make room for the young children of the Rose Hill Nursery.

December 1st - The final move of the nursery children took place today when they were taken from Styal to their newly built home in Longley Lane, Northenden.

1956

On 31st March 1956, the Homes were offically closed, but as the new family group homes situated on the housing estates at Wythenshawe. Blackley and Langley have not been available as quickly as was anticipated, it has been necessary to continue the use of seven cottages for the care of about forty children. It is expected that all the remaining children will have been transferred to their respective family group homes by the end of June.

The church organist Mr G.W. Taylor, the longest part-time employee of the Styal Homes, retired in March after 45 years service.

July 20th (Tuesday) 1956 - Bollin County Primary School Styal

"The last day in the life of the former Styal Homes Senior School. At mid-day the children were assembled for their last dismissal service. All the teachers, including Miss Bedford gave their good wishes. This is my last entry. It closes perhaps the volume - or perhaps only a chapter in the life of Bollin County Primary School. Signed: Norman Duffy"! School closed today for the summer vacation. As the remaining two children will be in a family group home before the beginning of the Autumn term, this school will not re-open.

Mr W.R. Barley, Superintendent for the final three years, gave his impressions in a summary and concluding report of the Styal Cottage Homes.

July 1956 - In many respects it has been a most depressing year,. The continued departure of boys and girls to the family group homes, unsettled staff and the knowledge that every main social event was to be the last one, all tended to make us feel very sad and to think that such a famous establishment which has produced so many worthy men and women was to close its gates for the last time.

The good tone of the homes has happily been maintained up to the end. The behaviour of the children both within and outside the homes has been exceptional with not one case of absconsion throughout the whole year. Much credit is due to the staff who have never spared themselves to give their children a happy home life and indeed much of their affections.

Throughout the last two years the children have enjoyed the hospitality of our immediate neighbours of Styal Village. In an interchange of invitations, the Fellowship Committee of Styal Village requested the presence of the children and staff of the homes to attend their socials, dances, evening lectures and sportsday activities. These have been much appreciated and enjoyed. The village community seem to be more aware of us and the work we are doing and the old cleavage between Homes colony and Village colony seems to have disappeared.

It has been my privilege to meet many ex-Styal boys and girls during the last three years, who have done extremely well in life. Amongst them have been a schoolmaster, company directors, musicians, Army Bandmasters, business owners, nurses and a chief welfare officer to quote only a few. They seem to come in their hundreds from all over the country and throughout the world, to visit their old homes'.

Whilst the Manchester Corporation were considering many suggestions regarding the future use of the Styal Estate including Summer Schools, temporary schools for Manchester children whose own schools were under modernisation programmes, etc,etc, a new crisis errupted with the arrival in this country of several thousand refugees, all victims of the 'uprising' in Hungary. During the month of December 1956, 800 refugees arrived at Styal and took up residence in the former Styal Homes Colony. Their temporary home lasted for two and a half years, approximately.

At the start of 1959 after a London based property tycoon had been refused permission to turn the Homes Estate into a luxury residential complex, the Home office Prison authorities informed the City Council that Styal would make an admirable type Open Air Borstal for Boys. Having received an official letter from the Home office, the Manchester Corporation approved the scheme for a Borstal on the condition that the Open Air School could be accommodated elsewhere. At a committee meeting on the 17th April, 1959 it was recommended that the Prison Commission use Styal Cottage Homes as a Borstal, subject to the Local and Planning Authorities. The terms were agreed to sell the Styal Homes to the Prison Commission on the 13th November 1959. By the end of the year the Prison Commissioners agreed to purchase Styal Cottage Homes for the sum of £70,000 and to designate its use as a Womens Prison.

The Manchester Residential Open Air School, adjacent to the Prison, was allowed to carry on with its role as an Open Air School for the treatment of delicate City children. Today, it is known as the 'Bollin Cross School'

Styal Homes Senior School known as Bollin County Primary School was sold to Wilmslow District Council for £6,000 in an exchange of land between Manchester Corporation and Wilmslow Council.

Sometime in the early 1960's, the modern school building was raised to the ground, with some of the timbers going to Quarry Bank Mill for the restoration programme. Only the iron school gates remain behind, and with them, the memories of a chapter of Styal's continuing history.

In presenting this biography - 'A Styal of its Own' - I have merely subscribed to the history of a village which, through one reason or another, finds itself one of the leading tourist attractions of the North West of England.

Like the novel 'A tale of two cities', Styal, from the beginning of the 20th century became a divided community, with the emergence of 'a village of two colonies'. If one were to insist that Edward Hyde Greg of Quarry Bank Mill, was responsible for this state of affairs, they would be justified in their assumption especially in light of all the evidence. On the other hand, one could argue that the Chorlton Guardians should shoulder the blame for choosing Styal as their base and promoting the hostility of E.H. Greg.

Leaving the politics of this issue to those better equipped, I prefer instead to adopt the view that once the Orphan Colony had established itself at Styal, one person more than anyone else was in the supreme position to accept or reject the unfortunate Withington children and to offer the milk of human kindness. History has shown the course which Mr Greg chose to pursue but what remains unclear is his decision, as founder member of Wilmslow District Council, to further isolate the Homes children by requesting the council members to refuse schooling facilities. Future generations of the Gregs of Styal appear to have followed the course set by Edward Hyde Greg, and the Norcliffe Farm saga only served to put the clock back for another 20 years. In 1954 the fraternization and social alliance between the Styal colonies had become firmly established. What a pity that 56 years had elapsed and thousands of children experienced a childhood without friend or affection. Discounting the Greg influence, a village resident commenting on his own experience, quoted; 'those big gates to the entrance of the colony, not only kept the boys and girls isolated but seemed also to serve as a deterrent to the villagers'.

When recalling past memories of childhood at the Styal Cottage Homes it must be remembered that many generations passed through the system and therefore a conflict of views was only natural, depending on which era and which staff, one relates to. Quite naturally some will testify to the happy childhood at Styal whilst most others will not hesitate to brand the institution as nothing short of a prison, where work schedules never ceased and cruel sadistic punishment was freely administered. In the main, it all depended on which cottage one resided and on the housemother who was in charge. As for the school teachers, it is the general view that they seemed to be fair in their general teaching, administration and punishment duties but there was one exception, namely Frederick Victor Smith, also known as 'Smiggy'. Many boys and girls can testify to this Headteacher who in his later years, bore all the hallmarks of a person who thrived on sadistic and perverse habits.

The strength of Styal Cottage Homes lay in its system of isolation, and with other contributary factors such as discipline and codes of conduct, the end product became a child who was unique. Come the day when adolescence demanded the departure from the Homes, all boys and girls who passed through the gates for the last time, carried with them the indelible stamp of the 'Styal syndrome'. This condition, acclaimed by the Manchester Children's Committee as 'institutionalism' could produce symptoms and mannerisms which lasted for up to four years after a child's release from the Home. Such was the unbelievable innocence and ignorance of the God-fearing 'Homes children' whose only possession on passing-out day was a Styal Homes Bible, the road from Styal to Adulthood became a tightrope where one slip could spell downfall and another, a stroke of good fortune. One can admit to the success of the authorities in their endeavours to provide security for the children, albeit at the price of institutionalism. Yet, one had to question the system which allowed children of such timidity to rejoin civilisation at their most vulnerable and tender years. In short, the Styal child was totally unprepared for the world which existed outside the colony and yesterday's security had become today's insecurity.

What has proved to be the most ironic circumstances in relation to the Styal Cottage Homes is its present day identity as Styal Prison. Throughout the history of the Homes in the generations of child residents, there has always been reference to the comparison of Styal

Homes to that of a prison. One particular piece of verse which echoed through the colony during the 1940–1952 period summed up the sentiments of the children of that era:-

'This time tomorrow we shall be
Out of the gates of misery,
No more sorrow no more pain
No more taste of Smiggy's cane'

My final reference to the Styal Homes rests with the distressing story of the War Memorial to the former boys of the Colony who died during the two world wars. Whilst researching 'A Styal of its own, I discovered to my amazement the disappearance of the two War Memorial tablets from the church of the former Homes, now Styal Prison. After an extensive period of letter writing to the Home Office, Styal Prison and the Church authorities, the whole exercise proved to be fruitless, each department admitting to a lack of knowledge to the existence of the two tablets. However, not to be deterred, the Manchester Evening News came to my assistance and through their famous 'Postbag' column I was rewarded with a genuine lead. Some weeks later I was in possession of the remains of one of the decorated War Memorial tablets. The story from that time on is too involved to relate in detail but I am satisfied to report a happy conclusion to an otherwise distasteful incident. With the co-operation of the Asst. Chaplain General (North) of the Home Office, and the Styal Village Farm Fold Methodist Chapel, the restored War Memorial tabloid was re-dedicated at a special Armistice Day service on 9th November 1986, to the memory of all the children of the Styal Cottage Homes.

One cannot escape the obvious irony of this episode which portrays the history of this once divided village. Farmfold Wesleyan Chapel has not only provided a final sanctuary for the former children of the Homes colony but has unintentionally brought them home to rest, in a quiet corner of Mr Greg's village and in full view of Greg's monumental Norcliffe Chapel.

In attempting to provide an epitaph to the Styal Homes Colony, I willingly admit to failure. The subject is too controversial, the participants too numerous, and socially and politically, I plead a qualified ignorance. I would prefer instead to quote the wisdom of the Stockport Mile End Guardians, who in 1899 said: "Apart from the excessive costs of the Homes, the children of Styal are too isolated from the rest of the world and therefore the scheme is impracticable".

Styal Village Colony on the other hand, has changed little during the past century and thanks to the National Trust, its preservation for the future is assured. Unlike the sleepy hamlet of yesteryear, Styal has adapted to it proximity to the bustle of Manchester's International Airport and yet, manages to retain the ability to hide behind the facade of a bygone era. Without doubt, the famous Quarry Bank Mill at Styal is the focal point of the village, with its acclaimed success attracting thousands of visitors from all over the world.